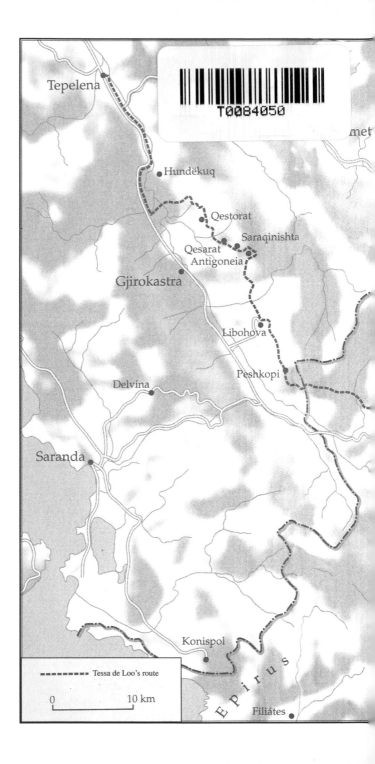

Tepelena

Hundëkuq

Qestorat

Saraqinishta

Qesarat
Antigoneia

Gjirokastra

Libohova

Peshkopi

Delvina

Saranda

Konispol

E p i r u s

Filiátes

T0084050

met

- - - - - - Tessa de Loo's route

0        10 km

Armchair Traveller
*at the* bookHaus

When Tessa de Loo saw Albania for the first time no foreigners were allowed to enter. Filled with a great curiosity, longing and a sense of wonderment at this isolated land, de Loo gazed toward the mountains that stood like "the backs of patiently waiting elephants" across the water from Corfu. Inspired by the famous Thomas Phillips portrait of Lord Byron in Albanian national costume, and enthralled by this image since her teenage years, she sets about not only exploring his physical journey, but also attempting to understand his inner one as well. de Loo stole her way in and found a country suffering the hardships of post-communist reality and the constant and sometimes fractious clash between tradition and modernity. In the tradition of Bruce Chatwin, de Loo, the award-winning author of *The Twins*, has written a fascinating travelogue and a very personal reassessment of a formative chapter in Lord Byron's short life.

# In Byron's Footsteps

by Tessa de Loo

Translated by Andy Brown

Armchair Traveller
at the bookHaus

# Foreword

MY DEAR GEORGE, it is not easy to accept that everyday life is the real life. Too often the sky is not blue or grey but filled with that indeterminate white that gives you a headache. The street in which you live seems straighter and duller than ever before, and even the magpie's nest in the sombre elm in front of your window seems part of a conspiracy to obstruct your desire to live, to really live. Why did the magpie build her nest in exactly the same place this year as last year? Does she not feel the ennui of routine?

The only place where anything of interest happens at all is in a luminous glass rectangle in the corner of the room, between 8.00 and 8.20 every evening (I can't possibly explain everything to you – please don't ask me to bring you up to date on the past two centuries). One evening, on that rectangular screen, the world watched as the Wall fell apart in thousands of pieces. People took the pieces home with them, to put on their mantelpieces or to sell as souvenirs.

In no time, the hordes came from the East in their little Trabants, with dollar signs in their eyes. And we went to take a look at how they had been living, with dollars in our pockets.

Was the Iron Curtain now really completely open? No, there was a country that was never seen on the glass rectangle, one country in Europe that didn't take part in the process of collective demystification. It stayed firmly closed, from the mountains in the north to the mountains in the south, from the coast in the west to the mountains in the east. Once, I had stood on the top of the Pantokrator on Corfu and looked to the east, intrigued by the massive grey hulks of the mountains on the other side of the narrow strait. They looked like the backs of patiently waiting elephants, if you reached out your hand far enough you could touch them. Only to pull it back again quickly, because what you did was forbidden.

The Land of the Skipetars. Karl May wrote books about countries that he had never visited. I imagine that he gathered as much information as he could from anywhere: geographical maps, topographic maps, travel guides, novels, dictionaries, history books, newspaper articles.

Because you have to start somewhere I bought a travel guide, a revised second edition from 1988. There was a Byzantine church on the cover, which helped a little to put me in the right mood. But Albania proved less mysterious than I had hoped. The guide covered all kinds of aspects of the country with no reserve at all: the geography, history, politics, the economy. It even described a number of tourist routes. Others had clearly gone before me. That was a pity – with things like this, as in love, you like to be the first and the only one.

I had nearly closed the book in disappointment when I happened to see a chapter entitled 'Lord Byron in Albania'. I discovered that you had been there, too, in 1809, together with your friend John Cam Hobhouse. The long letter you wrote to your mother about your journey was printed in full in the guide. I started to read. Although I still resisted, you drew me – in a way that appeared matter of fact, but in fact testified to an unremitting delight – into an Oriental world whose existence I had not suspected when I stood on the Pantokrator pondering the nature of the land beyond the grey mountains. I became enchanted by the exotic decor, the mishmash of peoples in their colourful costumes, the Pasha who could so easily show cruelty at one moment and tenderness the next, the call to prayer of the muezzin, the beat of the war-drums, the mixture of barbarism and refinement... And how, in the middle of all this, you allowed yourselves to be spoiled like two innocent children! It was almost impossible to believe that it was reality that you were describing in your letter and that the two of you had not had walk-on parts in some Eastern version of Macbeth.

Life in a staid street in Holland at the end of the 20th century could not compete with that. I wanted only one thing: to go with you. I wanted to visit Ali Pasha too, as a spectre from a future age, as a voyeur, as a nostalgia sufferer.

'My dear Mother,

I have now been some time in Turkey: this place [Prevesa] is
on the coast but I have traversed the interior of the province of
Albania on a visit to the Pacha. I left Malta in the *Spider*, a brig
of war, on the 21st of Septr. & arrived in eight days at Prevesa.
I thence have been about 150 miles as far as Tepaleen in his
highness's country palace, where I staid three days. The name of
the Pacha is Ali, & he is considered a man of the first abilities,
he governs the whole of Albania (the ancient Illyricum), Epirus,
& part of Macedonia, his son Velly Pacha to whom he has given
me letters governs the Morea & he has great influence in Egypt,
in short he is one of the most powerful men in the Ottoman
empire. When I reached Yanina the capital after a journey of
three days over the mountains through a country of the most
picturesque beauty, I found that Ali Pacha was with his army in
Illyricum besieging Ibrahim Pacha in the castle of Berat. He had
heard that an Englishman of rank was in his dominions & had
left orders in Yanina with the Commandant to provide a house
& supply me with every kind of necessity, *gratis*, & though I
have been permitted to make presents to the slaves &c. I have
not been permitted to pay for a single article of household
consumption. I rode out on the vizier's horses & saw the
palaces of himself & grandsons, they are splendid but too much
ornamented with silk & gold. I then went over the mountains
through Zitsa a village with a Greek monastery (where I slept
on my return) in the most beautiful Situation (always excepting
Cintra in Portugal) I ever beheld. In nine days I reached
Tepaleen, our Journey was much prolonged by the torrents
that had fallen from the mountains & intersected the roads.
I shall never forget the singular scene on entering Tepaleen at
five in the afternoon as the Sun was going down, it brought to
my recollection (with some change of *dress* however) Scott's
description of Branksome Castle in his *Lay*, & the feudal system.
The Albanese in their dresses (the most magnificent in the
world, consisting of a long *white kilt*, gold worked cloak, crimson
velvet gold laved jacket & waistcoat, silver mounted pistols &
daggers), the Tartars with their high caps, the Turks in their vast
pelises & turbans, the soldiers & black slaves with the horses,
the former stretched in groups in an immense open gallery in
front of the palace, the latter placed in a kind of cloister below

it, two hundred steeds ready caparisoned to move in a moment, couriers entering or passing out with the dispatches, the kettle drums beating, boys calling the hour from the minaret of the mosque, altogether, with the singular appearance of the building itself, formed a new & delightful spectacle to a stranger. I was conducted to a very handsome apartment & my health enquired after by the vizier's secretary "a la mode de Turque". The next day I was introduced to Ali Pacha, I was dressed in a full suit of Staff uniform with a very magnificent sabre &c. The vizier received me in a large room paved with marble, a fountain was playing in the centre, the apartment was surrounded by scarlet Ottomans, he received me *standing*, a wonderful complement from a Musselman, & made me sit down on his right hand. I have a Greek interpreter for general use, but a Physician of Ali's named [Seculario?] who understands Latin acted for me on this occasion. His first question was why at so an early age I left my country? (the Turks have no idea of travelling for amusement) he then said the English Minister Capt. Leake had told him I was of a great family, & desired his respects to my mother, which I now in the name of Ali Pacha present to you. He said he was certain I was a man of birth because I had small ears, curling hair, & little white hands, and expressed himself pleased with my appearance & garb. He told me to consider him as a father whilst I was in Turkey, & said he looked on me as his son. Indeed he treated me like a child, sending me almonds & sugared sherbet, fruit & sweetmeats 20 times a day. He begged me to visit him often, and at night when he was more at leisure. I then after coffee and pipes retired for the first time. I saw him thrice afterwards. It is singular that the Turks who have no hereditary dignities & few great families except the Sultan's pay so much respect to birth, for I found my pedigree more regarded than even my title. His highness is 60 years old, very fat & not tall, but with a fine face, light blue eyes & a white beard, his manner is very kind & at the same time he possesses that dignity which I find universal among the Turks. He has the appearance of any thing but his real character, for he is a remorseless tyrant, guilty of the most horrible cruelties, very brave & so good a general, that they call him the Mahometan Buonaparte. Napoleon has twice offered to make him King of Epirus, but he prefers the English interest & abhors the French as he himself told me, he is of so much consequence that he is courted by both, the Albanians being the most warlike subjects of the Sultan, though Ali is only nominally dependent on the Porte. He has been a mighty warrior, but is as barbarous as he is successful, roasting rebels &c. &c. Bonaparte sent him a snuff box with his picture[;] he said the snuff box was very well, but the picture he could excuse, as he neither liked *it* nor the *original*. His ideas of judging a man's birth from ears, hands &c. were curious enough. To me he was indeed a father, giving me letters, guards, & every possible accommodation. Our next conversations were of war & travelling, politics & England. He called my Albanian soldier who attends me, and told him to protect me at all hazards. His name is Viscillie & like all Albanians he is brave, rigidly honest & faithful, but they are cruel though not treacherous, & have several vices, but no meannesses. They are perhaps the most beautiful race in point of countenance in the world, their women are sometimes handsome also, but they are treated like slaves, *beaten* & in short complete beasts of burthen, they plough, dig & sow, I found them carrying wood & actually repairing the highways, the men are all soldiers, & war & the chase their sole occupations, the women are the labourers, which after all is no great hardship in so delightful a climate, yesterday the 11th. Nov. I bathed in the sea, today it is so hot that I am writing in a shady room of the English Consul's with three doors wide open no fire or even *fireplace* in the house except for culinary purposes.'

I recognised the palace of Ali Pasha as a place that I had always wanted to go to. And I recognised you, from when I was 16 and gazed mistily at the famous portrait of you in Albanian costume that was printed in my copy of 'Highroads of English of Literature' – and now again in the travel guide.

I remembered the fascination you held for me. As a poet whose lines seemed to mean more than they meant: 'My hair is gray, but not with years…' or 'I stood in Venice, on the Bridge of Sighs…' As a man full of contradictions, of strong emotions, of eternal rebellion. As a misanthropist. Young girls love misanthropists because they imagine that they are the only ones who can break through the armour with their guileless charm – Beauty and the Beast. As a sufferer of *Weltschmerz*: 'From my youth upwards, My spirit walked not with the souls of men…' As a fighter for freedom – I had just started to rattle my own chains. But my admiration for you was that of a besotted teenager. You were the object of my unattainable dreams. While my classmates exchanged pictures of James Dean, I peeked in my literature book at my beautiful dead poet.

And now, here I was, eye-to-eye with that same portrait and filled with the sudden desire – no, need – to travel with you. Where my revived interest and desire to be close to you came from, I did not ask. I did not wish to diminish the desire with reason. I wanted to leave it intact, cherish it, let it grow – and see where it would take me. Once again, I had been too sensible and too cautious for too long, why should I not allow myself to be led by the irrational, by a bizarre, unexpected need that came at me out of the blue?

I wanted to pick up where I had left off in my blind admiration: to get to know you better. And what better way than to go on a journey together? Perhaps I also wanted to find out why I had chosen you in particular as the projection of my dreams. And I needed that detour to find out who I was myself at the age of 16 – show me the object of your admiration and I will say who you are.

I silenced all those considerations. 'The deed justifies the desire' was my excuse for going off on a journey without asking myself what my motives were.

A lot of magpies' nests came and went before anything came of my plans. And in the meantime the situation had changed completely. Albania opened its borders and Europe responded by closing its own – to Albanians who tried desperately to flee their moribund country. It clearly wasn't very pleasant to live behind the waiting elephants after all. My life changed, too. I exchanged my straight Dutch street for a crooked country road in what you called 'that there Portingale'. You loved that country, too: 'I am very happy here, because I love oranges.'

Despite all the changes, my desire to go with you to the palace of Ali Pasha was in no way diminished. I began to make flanking movements, circling my ultimate goal. Although I have a deep aversion to clubs and associations, I joined the Byron Society in the Netherlands, a small group of admirers who keep your legacy alive. That meant that I was also automatically a member of the worldwide National Committee of the International Byron Societies, whose headquarters are in London. The president is also a Byron, and a distant relative of yours. Among the many vice-presidents, there is not a 'normal' person among them. There are Lords, Countesses, Viscounts, Reverends, Rt.

Honourables and Professors, every one of them from what you called 'that tight little island'.

These people organise trips for themselves and their fellow club members. When I heard that there was to be an international Byron congress in Athens in September, I thought: Why not, it's not so far from Albania?


IN ATHENS, the traffic ruled. For four nights I lay on my hotel bed, immobilised by noise, heat and lack of oxygen and yearning to close my eyes for an hour. Fortunately, there was plenty of opportunity to catch up on lost sleep during the lectures in the cool, neoclassical university building. The academics did not need my attention as they interpreted your poetry, full of passion. They were preaching to the converted.

This illustrious company included many weird and wonderful characters who one would not immediately associate with you. There was a lady professor from Armenia who spoke profusely and incomprehensively in the corridors, and gave an impression of complete chaos that was only reinforced by the loud, post-Communist flower pattern on her summer dress. In the midst of all the academic bustle, there was also a mysterious Japanese man, who observed everything with a tranquil Zazen smile. And, never far from the improvised bar, there was an American with cowboy boots and gangster sunglasses that he never took off, not even in the half-light.

A telephonist from Copenhagen confided to me, after a few glasses of Martini, that you regularly appeared to her to give her good advice. She told me that you had even requested she, so that she would be permanently at your disposal, give up her lover.

Delighted to have found someone who had an even more trivial relationship with you than I had, I asked: 'And, what did you do?'

'I finished with him immediately, of course!' she said, almost insulted. 'What did you expect?'

Cautiously I told her a little about my Albanian plan, though after her revelations the idea of going on a journey with you suddenly seemed to belong to the same sphere of unbridled idolatry and spiritism in which she, permanently slightly euphoric, seemed to move. My plan filled her with passion and awe: 'How I wish I could come with you both,' she sighed.

'First I want to find out what the risks are,' I said, backpedalling.

'Albania seems to me a country where your life is worth less than your wristwatch.'

But the telephonist was deaf to all protest. 'Just wait...' she said, laying a hand on my arm imploringly. 'Just leave it to me.'

The following morning she waved to me from far off. Before going to sleep she had consulted you to ask whether you would give your blessing to my plan. 'You can go on your journey with peace in your heart. He told me that nothing bad will happen to you .'

That was a great relief. But why did you never appear to me? Do you have to be a telephonist to be able to make such higher connections?

BY THE THIRD DAY I could no longer hold out. During a lecture on 'Historicity and scepticism in the 35th canto of *Don Juan*' I found myself fighting against sleep and the heat, tightly clamped between an incomprehensible Austrian and an elderly pink Irishman who lasciviously licked my ear at every opportunity, labouring under the delusion that he was unobserved. Had I come to Athens to sit in the lecture room of a university?

In the meantime I had read your collected travel letters and famous biography by Leslie Marchand and had become curious about the locations they referred to. Where, for example, was the house – not far from the Acropolis – where you had found shelter after your journey through Albania? The owner was the widow of a Greek who had been the British Vice-Consul. The widow, Macri, had three daughters all under 15, who you called 'the Three Graces'. You flirted so outrageously with the youngest, Theresa, that her mother had almost given her to you in marriage.

I wanted to find that house a thousand times more than to sit here dozing. Pretending I was going to faint, I crept outside. Outside I took a deep breath. Alone at last. I stopped a taxi and gave the driver the address – Odos Agias Theklas – as though nearly two centuries had not passed and you could still rent rooms at the widow's house. With a flush of pleasure I entered the street. I had the feeling that I had come improperly close to you, that at any moment I might step on your shadow.

I walked up and down the street, scouring the fronts of the houses for a plaque or some other sign that you had been here. An old man who saw me looking came to my aid, using his granddaughter as an interpreter. In broken English she told me that the house had been destroyed in an earthquake. She showed me the place where it had stood. The dilapidated interior walls were open to the world, displaying a variety of coloured plasterwork. The shelves of what had once been a cupboard were still nailed to one of them. Had your underwear lain there, in neat piles? According to Hobhouse, you had taken a large stock with you, as it would be difficult to wash them while you were travelling.

Why had the earthquake, out of this whole row, only destroyed the house of widow Macri? It seemed to have been carefully singled out. Everything that might have any connection with you was gone. An empty plot of land, empty walls, empty shelves – they simply made your absence even more emphatic. I had a foreboding that during our journey I would have to fill in many of the details, perhaps all of them, myself.


AMONG THE VISITORS to the congress I tried to find a member of the Albanian Byron Society. *The Byron Journal*, an annual periodical for members, mentioned a Professor Afrim Karagjozi, with a correspondence address in Tirana.

At a buffet dinner, while trying to juggle a fully-laden plate in one hand and a glass of wine in the other, I found myself standing next to Professor Raïzis, president of the Greek Byron Society and our host. He was an authoritative and seemingly amiable man with a voice that seemed to come from somewhere deep in his abdomen – an advantage when making speeches and official announcements.

I asked him where the Albanian delegation was. He frowned and told me curtly that his Albanian colleague had been unable to attend. Suddenly, as if there were a causal connection, he blurted out: 'Don't talk to me about Albania. It is a land of barbarians. The President, Berisha, belongs in a psychiatric institution... he is trying to incite war against Greece.'

This was clearly not a good moment to reveal my plans to travel to Tepelene. But I did anyway. Raïzis raised his eyebrows: 'Are you tired of living? Do you think you can just travel through that country? Alone? As a woman? Don't you know how the Albanians treat our women?'

His attention was distracted by another visitor and he turned his back on me. The retsina, never exactly nectar, was suddenly no longer to my taste. I put my half-full glass back among the full ones. Once again I had been reminded of my womanhood, as though it were some kind of shortcoming. That had started many years before: *'These are not girls' games, go and play with your dolls...'*

*'But I can throw knives as well as you...'*

The professor's warnings had only strengthened my resolve to go to Albania.

I DIDN'T KNOW then that I would have to return to the Netherlands to meet Karagjozi in person. And that I should be patient.

A year and a half later the Dutch Byron Society held its annual meeting in Amsterdam, in the fitting decor of the British Council building, a canal-side mansion decorated with Arcadian murals. A guest speaker had been invited who had retraced your footsteps through the northern Greek province of Epirus from Prevesa, where you had arrived by ship. My plan to travel with you was clearly not as absurd as it seemed.

The speaker immediately switched off the lights. The murals gave way to slides, which were equally Arcadian. My publisher, a member of the Society since time immemorial, had accompanied me as a favour. He took advantage of the darkness to take a nap. The first slide showed our speaker, carrying a heavy-looking pack and a shepherd's crook, moving jauntily along a goat track. He was surrounded only by hills and mountains, but this seemed not to bother him. There were more slides of unpaved roads, winding paths, half-collapsed bridges, and the ruins of fortifications or long-closed inns. Some of the slides were so life-like that you felt that you were really roaming around yourself in the dusty, mythical landscape in the copper-coloured light of the late afternoon sun. That was a pleasant sensation, as it was December outside and cold water flowed through the city's canals.

Of course, you were in our minds the whole time. Oh, how I envied and admired the speaker who had turned his wishes into deeds, on foot and with his belongings on his back. It could be that easy. You're my man, I thought. Still blissfully unaware of what lie in store, he continued his account, in a quiet, sonorous voice, and absent-mindedly, as though in his mind he was still there, in that distant place.

Afterwards, while the speaker was packing away his slides, my publisher hastily introduced me to someone called Gerda Mulder, who was about to leave. 'She knows all about Albania,' he whispered. Gerda Mulder pressed her card into my hand and hurried off. I later discovered that she had been one of the compilers of the Albanian Travel Guide, which had sparked off the whole adventure.

The members of the Society moved on to a nearby restaurant. Tables were pushed together and everyone tried to find a place. I waited until the guest speaker had sat down, and took possession of the chair opposite him. After he had had a few aperitifs to put him in the mood I invited him, during the Magret de Canard in orange sauce, to go to Tepelene with me. He did not hesitate for a moment, did not need to take a sip of wine or engage in any other form of displacement activity. With an amused and surprised smile, he immediately said 'Yes'.

My dinner companion was called Daniël Koster. He was a historian specialised in the modern history of Greece. He had lived on the island of Samos for five years and, when the season was favourable, worked on the land with the local farmers. So, luckily, he was not an ivory-tower academic, not a theorist who would spend his time staring up at the heavens, so that you would continually have to grab by him the collar to stop him from stepping over the edge of a precipice. He earned his living writing travel guides and articles about Greece. Twice a year, he would spend a few months walking on unmapped paths and writing about whatever he came across.

A telephone call to Gerda Mulder the next day put me on the trail of Professor Karagjozi. She told me he would be coming to the Netherlands to give a lecture in April. If I wanted to meet him, this was my chance. I was a little startled – my plan was starting to take shape. The telephonist from Copenhagen would have said that you had intervened personally, because everything was taking too long.

To find out more about the route of your journey I went to the University Library in Amsterdam, where I found an antiquarian copy of John Cam Hobhouse's account, illustrated with engravings. Hobhouse had resolved – and you secretly laughed at him for doing so – to keep an accurate record of the geography and topography of the landscapes you travelled through. I hoped that he would provide me with a reasonably reliable description of your route.

I had agreed with Daniël Koster that our own journey would start in the northern Greek town of Ioannina. It was there that you and Hobhouse had first entered the area controlled by Ali Pasha, and it was there that he had invited you to visit him in Tepelene.

Furthermore, we were both intrigued to learn more about Zitsa, your first stopping place after Ioannina, the beauty of which you praised so effusively in the letter to your mother. Hobhouse, too, was very impressed: 'The Prior of the monastery [...] entertained us in a warm chamber with grapes, and a pleasant white wine, not trodden out, as he told us, by the feet, but pressed from the grape by the hand; and we were so well pleased with every thing about us, that we agreed to lodge with him on our return from the Vizier.'

After reading your collected travel letters and a number of fragments from your diary, my former adoration was replaced by new perceptions. Then, I could never have suspected that you, the romantic poet of 'I stood in Venice, on the Bridge of Sighs', could be so astute and witty, that you would surprise me with your ruthless honesty and the self-knowledge it spawned – that you would so often make me burst into laughter. Engaging yet insufferable, noble yet malicious, a hedonist yet prone to melancholy, sensual yet austere – so many contradictions in one man, extremes that in you had become even more extreme. Reading you was a relief, you seemed to release me from the way I had become accustomed to dealing with my own ambiguity and duality. I have an ineradicable tendency to make peace, am always in the process of reconciling or disarming conflicts. Somewhere, in the vague middle ground, they have to dissolve into each other. It can be a real feat of strength. I sometimes think that my peacemaking is a veiled form of violence.

I admired you for the naturalness with which you dared, from a young age, to be yourself, to be authentic. In everything you did, you jumped in at the deep end. I am more the type who lies down flat on the diving board and spends a long time staring into the depths. My own tried and tested method of daring to do something is, without thinking, to climb the steps, run along the board, and jump off, eyes and nose held firmly closed. For me, that was the only way I could go to Albania.

FOUR MONTHS OF WAITING for a professor with a name that sounded like a nut cracking. I spent a lot of time leafing through my travel guide, which had been written before the fall of the Iron Curtain. More and more, I was amazed at the strange examples of Communist *couleur locale* I came across it its pages.

There was a report on an official visit by a group of foreigners to an infant school. The visitors would probably rather have been lying on the beach at Durrës, but the Albanian guide took a different view. The scenario was intended as propaganda, but to a tourist from the West it sounded more like a caricature from a satirical comedy show:

'The head of the school welcomes the visitors at the entrance and takes them to a classroom, where a group of at least 20 children are waiting patiently. Both the boys and the girls wear white aprons. The visitors are treated to a programme of songs, poems and dance, often performed with great energy and enthusiasm. Promising to do her very best, a small girl reads a verse for Enver Hoxha. A young boy declares that he will later become a soldier and defend his socialist fatherland by welcoming anyone who crosses its borders uninvited with a bullet through the head. Then all the children sing a song about sunflowers, which they have to water every day, but which they are not permitted to keep as they are a gift for 'Uncle Enver'. A few boys and girls do a dance, holding wooden pickaxes and guns – symbols of the development of their country.'

I hoped that I would never meet the boy, who may now have become a soldier, as we ourselves crossed the border into his homeland. I also hoped that, on the way, we would be able to rely on the traditional Albanian hospitality described in the guide: 'The guest was sacred and there were all kinds of rules for receiving visitors, such as washing their feet, relieving them of their weapons, and offering them food and drink and a place to sleep. The law of hospitality went so far that two men involved in a vendetta, and who would therefore have to kill each other outside, could sit and drink raki together calmly in the house of a third party.'

We would be completely at the mercy of those rules of hospitality. It was unlikely that, since your journey – the rigours of which Hobhouse described so expansively – the foothills of Mount Lunxheris would have changed much. That was the attraction of the region – that hopefully nothing would have changed. No asphalt roads, like everywhere else in Europe. No hotels, guesthouses or restaurants. No facilities at all for the traveller, and the concept of 'tourist' still unknown. We would be the first travellers since the fall of the Ottoman Empire! Your journey, in fact, marked the end of the Grand Tour and the birth of tourism, a word first used in 1814 by a journalist in the Quarterly Review, in an article on the popularity that Greece was suddenly enjoying among travellers. Travel was no longer the monopoly of aristocrats – the advent of industry had led to the rise of a new middle class who also wanted to see what it was like on the other side of the English Channel. The consequences that tourism has had since then for the state of the world, even for its most unspoiled regions, you cannot possibly imagine.

In April, I finally met him face to face. Afrim Karagjozi was sitting across the table from me in the first-class restaurant at Amsterdam Central Station. Unconsciously I had formed an image of a man with stubble on his face, his skin tanned by the sun and a bullet belt around his middle, like the Albanians in the prints in Hobhouse's book. But the professor was a small, pale, middle-aged English specialist. Long ago he had written his thesis on your journey through Albania. Although he had been born in Gjirokastër, the town that you continually saw from the mountainside but never visited, he was never given permission to take a look at the route on which his thesis was based: for many years Albanians were not allowed to travel freely through their own country.

I revealed my plan. Karagjozi beamed. 'It is a fantastic idea,' he said. Would he like to accompany us, as a dragoman, the leader of a literary expedition, a traveller in his own thesis? The professor did not hesitate for a second. Before I had finished speaking, he was nodding delightedly. It would be a great pleasure for him to accompany us. He felt it only honest to tell me that, many years previously, he had had problems with his heart. He had had an attack and spent several days in a coma. It had been caused by emotional problems, he said, adding: 'I have had a very difficult life.' But since he had stuck to a strict diet and took a walk round the park in Tirana every day, he had been much better. He was now 55, and was in excellent health.

'Can you ride a horse?' I asked.

He looked at me in amazement.

'It would be appropriate,' I continued, 'and completely in Byron's style, to travel through Albania on horseback.'

For a moment, he was silent, staring at the glass of wine in his hand. The he said softly, 'If it is necessary, I will also climb up onto the back of a horse.'

'Will we be able to get horses?' I asked.

He shook his head. 'No problem.'

'And accommodation?'

'I'll handle this, don't worry.'

Later, during in the journey, these words would become something of a mantra, an incantation when the going got rough. The professor dismissed any practical problems I suggested with a cheerful 'No problem'. From the twinkle in his eyes I could see that he was not afraid to take on the great responsibility of ensuring the safety of two Dutch travellers in the mountainous regions of his fatherland. Regions rendered unsafe by brigands since time immemorial, full of deep ravines where you could make someone disappear without trace.

And so it was decided.

# Chapter 1

O
N 2 JULY in the year 1809 a packet boat left the port of Falmouth, in southwest England, for Lisbon. On board was George Gordon Byron, determined never to return to his native country. He was 21 years old, had just graduated from Cambridge, and had a seat in the House of Lords where, insulted at his delayed admission, he had demonstratively sat in the benches of the Whigs – an early indication that he was 'born for opposition'. He had already achieved his first literary success. The publication of *English Bards and Scotch Reviewers*, which had been received by a number of caustic reviews dismissing his verses as 'school exercises'. Byron was so enraged – to the point of self-destruction, according to a friend – he had almost challenged the publisher of the reviews to a duel.

Plagued by money problems, he had awaited his departure for many months. While he was studying he had succeeded in accumulating a debt of 13,000 pounds. To settle that and to raise funds for his voyage, he had ordered his business agent John Hanson to sell the family estate Rochdale, saying: '[...] allow me to depart from this cursed country, and I promise to turn Mussulman, rather than return to it.' Eventually the money for the journey was advanced by his friend, fellow student and companion in indulgence Scrope B. Davies, after the latter had spent a profitable evening at the gaming table.

The intention was to make a Grand Tour to the classical locations in Italy, Greece and Turkey, as was customary among young, newly graduated aristocrats. Byron may have taken his seat in the House of Lords among the Lower Classes, but he travelled as a lord. What and who did he take with him? In addition to an impressive assortment of travelling equipment, which can best be described as a portable household, there was the old family servant Joe Murray, his valet

William Fletcher, who would remain loyal to Byron until his death, and the handsome page Robert Rushton. He also took along as a travelling companion John Cam Hobhouse, a dear friend from Cambridge who shared his love of literature. It was Hobhouse's ambition to record the shared journey in detail. Byron remarked ironically: 'Hobhouse has made woundy preparations for a book at his return, 100 pens two gallons Japan Ink, and several vols best blank is no bad provision for a discerning Public.' He declared to have few plans of that nature himself: 'I have laid down my pen, but have promised to contribute a chapter on the state of morals, and a further treatise on the same to be entitled 'Sodomy simplified or Paederasty proved to be praiseworthy from ancient authors and modern practice.'

WE SHALL NEVER KNOW to what extent Byron intended in advance to conduct empirical research for his work based on his own experience in the Orient, but we do know that his pen was not still for long. Inspired by the journey, he would write the epic poem *Childe Harold's Pilgrimage*, which caused such a sensation that 'one day he awoke to find himself famous'.

And so they departed. Most English travellers commenced their Grand Tour in France but Byron and his company took a diversion to Portugal to avoid the Napoleonic wars. After a stay of 14 days, they travelled overland to Seville, Cadiz and Gibraltar. Their further plans depended on the wind.

'I am going over to Africa tomorrow,' Byron wrote on 11 August, as if it were the most normal thing in the world; but two days later, he had still not left. 'I have not yet been to Africa, the wind is contrary, [...] General Castanos, the celebrated Spanish leader in the late & present war [...] has offered me letters to Tetuan in Barbary for the principal Moors [...].' Another two days later, he had had enough of waiting: 'I cannot go to Barbary, the Malta packet sails tomorrow & myself in it.' Joe Murray was sent home with the page: 'I would have taken him on but you *know boys* are not *safe* amongst the Turks.'

FROM MALTA A WAR BRIGANTINE that accompanied British merchant ships took them to Prevesa, on the Greek coast. En route, they moored in Patras, where Byron felt 'Greek soil under his feet' for the first time. He marked this event, so exciting for someone who knew and cherished his classics, with a volley of pistol shots. On the way to Prevesa they also saw to the north, on the far side of the Gulf of Lepanto, the marshy city of Missolonghi where, 15 years later, Byron would die in miserable circumstances. But now he was young and unsuspecting. And innocent, you might say almost automatically, but then – knowing him – you would swallow your words just as quickly.

The company went ashore in Prevesa on 29 September. They had donned the uniforms of their regiment for the occasion, but they soon became soaked by the rain as they trudged through the muddy streets between the squalid houses. Byron was well-equipped to deal with all kinds of discomfort, but Hobhouse admitted honestly that, on his first day on Greek soil, he wanted nothing more than to turn around and go back to 'Good Old England'. After hiring a dragoman, they left for Ioannina on 1 October. This was when they first heard the name of Ali Pasha, a powerful Albanian ruler who answered directly to the Sultan. Ioannina was the brand new capital of Ali's empire, which he had accumulated by looting and pillaging. It extended in the north to include half of present-day Albania, to the east nearly to Thessaloniki, and in the west to the coast. To the south, it also embraced the Morea, now known as the Peloponnesus.

They hired ten horses for 35 piasters. Four for themselves, Fletcher and the dragoman, four for the baggage, and two for the soldiers who were responsible for their safety. There was much to lug around with them: a large quantity of linen, four leather trunks full of books, two smaller trunks, a canteen, three beds and two light wooden bed-steads, as a precaution against vermin and damp floors. Hobhouse was particularly fond of all these trappings, as they were very benefi-cial to his comfort and health. He also noted how fortunate it was that they had brought their own saddles and bridles from home, as the wooden pack-saddles of the Turkish post horses were torture for the seat of an Englishman.

Four days later, Ioannina appeared before them in the distance. Hobhouse described his first impression: 'The houses, domes and minarets, glittering through gardens of orange and lemon trees, and from groves of cypresses – the lake spreading its smooth expanse at the foot of the city – the mountains rising abruptly from the banks of the lake – all these burst upon us.'

They rode into the city, enchanted by so much Oriental beauty. They passed one of the Vizier's (Ali Pasha) new houses, a number of

Turkish tombstones and shops. Hanging on the boughs of a large tree opposite a butcher's shop was something that, from a distance, looked like a piece of meat that was for sale. From close up, it proved to be a man's arm, with part of his torso still attached. It was hanging by a string tied around the fingers. Hobhouse commented that they should not too quickly condemn the Turks for being barbarians. The arm later proved to belong to a rebel who had been beheaded five days earlier. His other remains were on show in various parts of Ioannina, as an example and for entertainment.

The friends made their way to the house of the English resident, William Leake, for whom they had a letter from the Governor of Malta. They discovered that comfortable lodgings had already been arranged in the house of a hospitable Greek called Niccolo Argyri, who had lived in Trieste for several years and spoke fluent Italian.

There is a famous print of this house. On the ground floor you can see the arched entrances to the stables. An ornamentally carved wooden staircase leads to the first floor, which is the living area. Three men sit amiably together, cross-legged. A minaret in the distance, a horse, a peacock with a long, hanging tail, and a pipe-smoker in a fez in the foreground give the scene an intimate, rural atmosphere. You feel as though you could just step into it, though I would probably be sent immediately to the women's quarters.

Before long, the Vizier's secretary came to congratulate them on their safe arrival. The rumour of the arrival of two young Englishmen had already reached the Pasha, and he had issued orders for everything to be prepared to make them as comfortable as possible. Unfortunately he was unable to receive them personally because he was in the north finishing a small war. He invited the friends, however, to visit him at his palace in Tepelene and, according to Hobhouse, 'an escort was provided for that purpose, to be ready at our command'.

# Chapter 2

M Y DEAR GEORGE, in 1809, you had to wait weeks for a favourable wind before embarking on a long sea voyage. On 11 September 1996, we travelled from Amsterdam to Ioannina in a single
day – by land, by sea and through the air.

We took off in Amsterdam in the morning and a few hours later,
we landed in Corfu. We crossed to Igoumenitsa not on a war brigantine, but in a ferryboat. It was not worth us donning our regimental
uniforms for our arrival at this unappetising little port, and we left it
as soon as possible by bus. Our uniform was that of the backpacker.
A rucksack is easier to bind to a horse than a plastic Samsonite.
Moreover, the poorer our convoy appeared on our journey through
Albania, the better, The only notable feature about the company was
Daniël's shepherd's crook, which gave him a kind of apostolic dignity.

Few towns at the end of the 20th century allow themselves to be
described in the idyllic words of Hobhouse. A modern city is like an
over-ripe fruit. The peel and the pulp are the usually hideous suburbs
that you have to make your way through to get to the stone – the
old centre which, if you are lucky, will not have been completely
destroyed by the unquenchable drive to modernise. Domes, minarets, church spires, once beacons for the traveller, are lost among
towers of concrete and steel, which seem to tempt God's wrath by
reaching so recklessly towards His heaven.

In Ioannina, too, the bus picked its way through the ugliness. We
had no desire to stay the night there. Wouldn't it have been wonderful if the Pasha, hearing of the arrival of two Hollanders, had arranged
accommodation for us in the house of a rich, cosmopolitan Greek?
But we had to do everything ourselves and hurried to the banks of
Lake Pamvotis to take the boat to the island of Nissaki, which may
officially be part of Ioannina, but in practice is completely separate.

Daniël remembered from one of his previous visits that there was a quiet guesthouse there.

In your time, you simply travelled along with yourself, but in our time our bodies are transported quickly, together with our baggage, from place to place. Our prehistoric mind, which cannot travel faster than on foot, or at most by horse, follows on behind slowly and unwillingly. Sometimes it refuses to come at all, especially on short, spectacular holidays. When we arrive back at home, we find it sitting by the fireside, and as soon as we are rejoined, the holiday appears to be a vague dream and our behaviour in exotic parts that of a stranger.

The island in the lake at Ioannina has traditionally been known as the navel of Epirus. Perhaps Ali Pasha tried to crawl back along the umbilical cord and into the womb when he hid himself from the Sultan's soldiers in the small monastery of St. Panteleimonas, where they ultimately managed to find him. The monastery's patron saint could not prevent them, 13 years after your visit, from killing and decapitating him. Our guesthouse was only 100 footsteps away from the monastery. I hoped that the 'fine face' with the 'light-blue eyes & white beard' – in other words, the Pasha's head, separated from his shoulders – would not appear to me at night in my deepest sleep.

We took an evening walk. The only village, allegedly built by refugees from Mani in the 17th century, is no more than a clump of white houses, with roofs of flat, lead-coloured stones. There is still a feeling of rustic tranquillity, despite the few streets with souvenir shops offering fake water pipes and plaster casts of Venus and Apollo. Between the shops are restaurants with aquaria in front, in which eels, trout, crayfish and frogs swim lazily in murky water. Hopeful waiters repeatedly stopped us and, pointing to an aquarium, tried to entice us to sample their wares. But we had both seen the colour of the lake, which was fluorescent green from algae. It was strangely still, as though it were on the point of death. Yet, from the wooden rowing boats that could be seen everywhere between the reeds, the majority of the island-dwellers still seemed to make a living from fishing. According to a tourist leaflet, the eels from Lake Pamvotis are a renowned export product, as are the frogs, which are particularly popular in France: *Cuisses de Grenouilles aux Alges*.

Fortunately, the largest part of the village had remained unspoilt. There were no cars. The streets were paved with flat stones polished by many feet. It was quiet that evening on Nissaki, something that is very rare in our century. The late sunlight fell upon scenes that are timeless. You would not have wasted words on them, but Hobhouse would have described them all in great detail: brightly coloured flower gardens, weeping willows, sheep, goats, cats, widows in black feeding the chickens, large woodpiles, and here and there the smell of a fire.

I had never before seen such large plane trees. Some were said to be more than 500 years old. I used to associate planes with peaceful squares in Provence, but since I had become acquainted with the history of Albania and Ali Pasha, they now made me think of sinister punishments. 'In 1809,' reported a brochure about Ioannina, 'Ali Pasha tortured the leader of the rebels, Katsdantonis and his brother Chasiotis beneath a plane tree near his palace.' And the Albanian Travel Guide told of two young women who had fought in the resistance against the Nazis and were hanged in 1944 from the branches of a plane in the great square in Gjirokastër. The Dutch writer and painter Armando devised the term 'guilty landscape' for spots in the country that had been besmirched by horrific atrocities during the Second World War; here, you could say there were 'guilty trees'. During my journey, however, the planes retrieved their innocence for me when I saw whole forests of them in the valleys of mountain streams. Under their wide, light-green leaf canopies, the filtered sunlight produced a *Déjeuner sur l'Herbe* atmosphere.

Because it does not seem to be part of the rest of the world, the island of Nissaki has held a great attraction for monks and hermits since the Middle Ages. During our short walk, we passed five monasteries, which nestled against the mountainside and, with their intimate inner courtyards, created an impression that a life of purity and beauty should be possible. Saints with illustrious names protected the monasteries: Michael Philantropinon, St. Panteleimonas, St. Ioannis Prodromos, Ayios Eloussa and Stratigopoulos. The monks had aroused the spirit of resistance among the Greeks to free themselves from Turkish domination – but I do not need to tell you about their struggle. There used to be a secret school in the 13th-century monastery above the village, founded by the *Philantropinoi*, six brothers and cousins who, as philosophers and teachers, propagated their ideals of humanity, education and freedom in a world that was not ready for them, and perhaps never will be.

When we reached the west side of the island I came to a halt, overwhelmed. Before me, the scene revealed itself, unspoiled, that Hobhouse had seen and described on approaching Ioannina: the sun set behind 'the houses, domes and minarets, glittering through gardens of orange and lemon trees'. From here, across the water, we could see the old silhouette of the citadel, the Frourion, where you visited one of Ali's palaces and were received with the greatest respect by his grandson, who was looking after the house while his grandfather was in Tepelene. My head was overfull from all the accounts I had read about this region. They tumbled over each other in their eagerness to have new life breathed into them – here, and nowhere else, they had all been played out.

That evening, despite a loud conversation being conducted under my bedroom window, I fell asleep immediately. I just heard Daniël's angry voice as he called from his own window: 'There are people here trying to sleep!' Outside the café next door, the men of the village were sitting and discussing the business of the day, as they have done since time immemorial: with much raising of voices and displays of masculinity. Every pavement café in Greece is still a Stoa in miniature.

'What were they talking about?' I asked Daniël at breakfast. He shrugged his shoulders. 'Politics. Money.'

Five years on Samos and countless walks through the country had destroyed any illusions he may have had about the ancient wisdom of the Greeks. They were always right, he said, without being troubled by actually knowing what they were talking about. He had long ago given up entering into discussion with them about anything; every attempt foundered on nationalism, boasting and historical ignorance.

'Perhaps they need a new Socrates,' I suggested.

'He would go the same way as his predecessor,' Daniël replied sombrely.

We crossed back over the green lake. Daniël, who knew Ioannina from previous visits, went off to visit the ethnographic museum. Suddenly I was alone on the quay, the day lay before me – but my impatience to see everything paralysed my resolve.

The memory of the silhouette of the mosque set me in motion again. I walked along the wall that encircled the citadel, looking for an entrance gate. Opposite a row of cafés and restaurants I found a half-dark gateway, the length of which betrayed the thickness of the wall. Tunnels are mostly symbols of death and rebirth – leaving the old, familiar world and entering a new one – but for me, it was vice-versa. I left the new world to enter the old one, an underworld where I hoped to find you and Hobhouse and Ali Pasha and all those

Albanians, armed to the teeth – like a Scheherazade on the way to the place where she must try to extend her life by telling stories.

The tunnel filtered out the 20th century, with all its hubbub. I breathed again. There was no traffic in the narrow alleyways. I walked through a domain of old people, children, cats and birds. I did my best to recognise the houses of the past in the not-very-conscientiously restored buildings. I could see from the bay windows that people used to live on the first floor. On the ground floor were the entrance, the stairs and the stables. Many of the windows were protected by bars; the times had always been dangerous and who knows what the future holds?

Emerging from an alley I found myself in a space that demanded respect for the sight that rose up from behind the leafy crowns of deciduous trees and the black needles of cypresses: the mosque. The light of the sun gave it an autumnal sharpness. A vulnerable sanctum that had survived fire, destruction and human passion. It was somehow moving that it was still there. Oriental decoration and a comforting balance between horizontal, vertical and round lines. A minaret and a cypress seemed to be reaching up to heaven in a rivalry that only Allah can settle.

Why did you, George, not visit the mosque on your way to Ali's palace? Did the idea not occur to you, or was it not permitted for Christian infidels to do so? I entered hesitantly, not sure if, as a woman, I *was* permitted and whether I should leave my shoes near the entrance. But my concerns proved unfounded – the mosque proved to be a museum open to everyone, with a large collection of weapons and costumes. Weapons in a house of God? The Turkish swords used to win the Holy War felt completely at home there. But the weapons which the Greeks used to try and drive out the Turkish occupiers seemed less at ease.

I stared at the enormous sword of a Greek soldier called Baka from Pramanda who, according to the explanatory text, had helped to defend Missolonghi. Do you happen to remember a soldier called Baka? From when you were waiting endlessly until you could see action with your Suliote corps? Soldier Baka with his enormous sword, its hilt inlaid with ivory? Do you know what fate befell him after your death? During the second exodus from Missolonghi, when the last citizens fled from the approaching Turks, he was captured, along with six other soldiers. The museum says nothing of what happened to him after that. Was there an 'after' at all, once you were in a Turkish prison?

I wandered into the costume section. Gaping at the clothes of a dead person has something improper, even necrophilic about it. Clothes are intimate, perhaps they still carry the scent of their dead wearers, or the shapes of their elbows or knees. I hate to think of complete strangers commenting on my best dress 100 years after my death. Who knows what they themselves might be wearing?

Slightly embarrassed, I looked at expertly woven and embroidered skirts and blouses, until I was standing in front of the costume of a Suliote woman. What did the wives of the most renowned warriors of the last century wear? A cream-coloured underskirt, with an embroidered skirt and a knee-length vest, set off by an imposing belt and a necklace of silver filigree. Around her head she wore a black scarf, and on her feet Turkish shoes with large red pom-poms. Everything was red and black, the colours of life and death. Quite farsighted, you might think, given the reason Suliote women have become so legendary.

The Suliotes were Albanian Christians. They lived on the foothills of Lightning Mountain, not far from Ioannina, on a number of unassailable rocky plateaus. They kept sheep and goats, but because nothing grew in the rocky ground, they lived by looting and pillaging, which was a thorn in the side of Ali Pasha, who wanted a monopoly on those particular activities for himself. For many years, the Suliote warriors succeeded in repelling Ali's attacks. But in 1803, the war of attrition had defeated them and they had to surrender.

Their women died rather than face rape and slavery. They fled to the highest rocks and jumped to their deaths, together with their children. It is told that they first danced and sang songs, in a whirl of black and red, a *dance macabre* in which they waltzed playfully, holding their struggling children, into the underworld. You knew this story of course, because you had a weakness for these people who, like you, chose freedom above everything. You did not know, when you took on a bunch of these half savages to help you fight the decisive battle against the Turks, that you would have your hands full. I believe that you were so disappointed and morally undermined by them that they were at least partly responsible for your death.

I pushed the display cabinets full of weapons and costumes out of my thoughts and concentrated on the interior of the mosque. It is a miracle that the citizens of Ioannina, most of them Greeks, did not raze the building to the ground when the Turks were driven from the region in 1813. After all, less than a century before, the Turks had done the same with Ali Pasha's palaces – symbolic destruction of the relics of power was an ancient custom. Turning the mosque into a museum was a more tactical solution.

There were no more Turks on their knees on prayer mats, no more muezzin calling them to prayer. The last of the Turks had long ago flown home on their magic carpets to make new concessions in their shrunken empire. And yet, the religion they had practised was still visible everywhere. In the architecture, in the absence of human or animal images, in the arabesques that replaced them. Later, when I saw Byzantine churches full of gilded iconostases, I especially remembered the pleasing simplicity of this mosque. It was as though less effort had been made to impose and more to inspire trust.

I left the high, domed mosque. It was time to take a look at the fortress, known by the Turks as Its Kale. I passed a library, a low building with three slated domes. Ali Pasha, who could neither read nor write, had probably never seen it from the inside. Next door there was a bathhouse. The roof was covered in parched grass. The building looked as though it had been closed for centuries because it was in danger of collapse. Do you remember that you and Hobhouse wanted to go in one evening, but were frightened off at the entrance by an old masseur? Your host, Signor Niccolo Argyri, later expressed his regret at this incident as, in the interior where the actual washing took place, you would have been served by 'belli Giovanni'.

A large gateway provides access to the expansive site that was once the domain of the Pasha. It was hot – the buildings that had once provided shadow were no longer there. This was historic ground about which the Greek folder I carried proclaimed effusively: 'How much was every spot here, every molecule, drenched with blood! How many fountains of tears were spilled over this land for many centuries!' And then, a touch of modern-day patriotism: 'You feel pity, but also pride, and your spirit whispers to you from within.'

Without much enthusiasm I clambered over the ruins of half collapsed walls and domes. A few casemates were still intact and part of a Byzantine tower known as the Thomas Tower. Attempts at restoration had been abandoned. It was too much for my imagination and the sun burned down mercilessly. Even those who had died here with a rope around their necks had at least been hanged in the shadow of a plane tree. That thought alone automatically took me in the direction of the tree under which Katsantonis and his brother Chasiotis had died a slow death.

Hobhouse tells the story differently: 'A few months before our arrival in the country, a large body infesting the mountains between Ioannina and Triccala, were defeated and dispersed by Mouctar Pasha, who cut to pieces a hundred of them on the spot. These robbers had been headed by a Greek Priest, who, after the defeat of his men, went to Constantinople, procured a firman of protection, and returned to Ioannina, where the Vizier invited him to a conference, and seized him as he was leaving the room. He was detained, and well treated in prison, until a messenger could go and return from Constantinople, with a permission from the Porte for Ali to do what he pleased with his prisoner. – It was the arm of this man which we had seen suspended from the bough, on entering Ioannina.'

Strangely enough, the brother does not appear in this account. Such treachery from the Vizier! And the Sultan was no better. A man a man, a word a word – this clearly did not apply in the Ottoman Empire. You could trust no one. The naive leader of the rebels should have known that. There is a print dating from 1820 showing a group of rebels dancing on the shores of Lake Pamvotis, their guns raised at their shoulders. Their morale appears not to have been broken by the execution of their leaders. It looks as though they are on the island, as the view of the mosque across the water is identical to the one we saw during our evening walk.

I found the tree that had seen so much. It had survived everyone and stood there as though there was nothing to be concerned about. Ali Pasha's grave was nearby – or rather, the remains of the grave in which his headless body had been buried. Where his palace had once stood there was now, bare and joyless, a clumsy imitation. It was a dour stone rectangle, that had nothing in common with Ali's flamboyant seraglio as it is depicted in the engravings and which you described with these words: 'I [...] saw the palaces of himself and grandsons; they are splendid but too much ornamented with silk and gold.'

You especially had much to say about the grandsons, who did not yet know that, 13 years later, they would be punished for their grandfather's insatiable desire to conquer new territories: 'I have been introduced to Hussein Bey, and Mahmout Pacha, both little boys, grandchildren of Ali at Yanina. They are totally unlike our lads, have painted complexions like rouged dowagers, large black eyes and features perfectly regular. They are the prettiest little animals I ever saw, and are broken into the court ceremonies already. The Turkish salute is a slight inclination of the head with the hand on the breast, intimates always kiss. Mahmout is ten years old and hopes to see me again, we are friends without understanding each other, like many other folks, though from a different cause.'

Thank God there was a café near the gate. I sat at an outside table in the shade and ordered water, a lot of water. Next to me, there was a group of young boys with a ghetto-blaster from which Greek pop music blared. They were only a few years older than Hussein and Mahmout. They were not wearing rouge, and did not have features perfectly regular but, naturally, they were also wild animals. It was as though, after Ali's fall, the world here had ceased to exist and then, *tabula rasa*, had started again with a completely different species of human being, and against a different backdrop. I had resolved, for the duration of the journey, to mediate between these two worlds – to join them with a cord, on which I wobbled uncertainly, a brightly-coloured parasol on one hand to help me keep my balance and to break my fall if I lost it. The imagination as a parachute. Why was the confrontation with a lost world so painful? Was it my own mortality that hampered me?

Hobhouse chatters light-heartedly about the visits you made. On the second day after your arrival in Ioannina, you went to a palace that Ali Pasha had given to his oldest son, Mouctar. Because his father was absent, you were welcomed by Ali's grandson: '[...] and he received us, though he was a boy of only ten years old, with a polite unembarrassed air, desiring us, with a gentle motion of his hand, to sit down near him. His preceptor, a grave old man, with a beard reaching to his knees, sat in the corner opposite to him, but did not interfere in the conversation. The Bey, for that was his title, though he was a little inquisitive as to some parts of our dress, and was highly delighted by a handsome sword worn by my Friend, yet preserved his dignity and gravity, nor could we observe but very little difference between his manners and those of his aged tutor.'

After coffee and sweetmeats, you expressed the wish to see the palace. It was possible, but first your small host ordered his father's wives to withdraw to the inner apartments of the harem. On leaving the room, he was tenderly embraced by a shabbily dressed Albanian guard. Hobhouse noted that the people's attitude towards the boy was 'a singular mixture of familiarity and respect'.

I would love to know what the palace looked like from the inside. You are very brief: splendid, but too much silk and gold. I do not wish to imply that Hobhouse saw more than you but, as befits the amateur ethnographer that he wished to be, he records more than you – all kinds of details that you dismiss as uninteresting. He found the rooms handsomely and comfortably furnished, especially those used during the winter. With silk-upholstered sofas, the best Turkish carpets, windows of Venetian glass. He did not, however, always approve of the wainscots: 'In one compartment was a tawdry representation of Constantinople, a favourite subject, and one which we recognised in almost every painted house in Turkey.' Did kitsch exist in your time, too? Although one of the rooms had a recess with a bath and a fountain, there were no bedrooms because the Turks used all the rooms for sleeping. Each room had a cupboard containing mats and blankets, that were laid on the floor at night.

Little Bey was delighted to show you his father's palace, and every now and again, he would lose his reserve. He told you that he spoke Albanian and Greek, and was now learning to speak and write Turkish and Arabic – in that respect he had already left his illiterate grandfather far behind. Hobhouse, who was continually amazed at the level-headedness and politeness of Ali's grandsons, discovered during his stay that the children of all the better Mohammedan families had such good manners.

And then the apple of your eye, Mahomet. He was staying here in Its Kale during your visit and was taking care of his grandfather's palace. According to Hobhouse, Mahomet was much more lively than Hussein. It was said that he had inherited Ali Pasha's genius. Although he was only ten years old, he already had his own *pashalik*. 'He did the honours with the same ease as his cousin, and after sitting a short time, proposed a visit to a younger brother of his, who was at a house belonging to their father'. Now and again, it makes you dizzy, all that back and forth between all the family's palaces.

'A messenger was sent before us, and we set out on horses caparisoned with gold housings, whilst some officers of the palace, with their wands and silver sticks, preceded us. As the young Pasha passed, through the streets, all the people rose from their shops, and those who were walking stood still, every body paying him the usual reference, by bending their bodies very low, touching the ground with their right hands, and then bringing them up to their mouths and foreheads (for the adoration of the great is, in its primitive and literal sense, still preserved among the Orientals). The Bey returned the salute by laying his right hand on his breast, and by a gentle inclination of the head.'

What a brat, you might think at the end of the 20th century, when princes are brought up to be 'as normal as possible'. But this brat's grandfather had the power over life and death.

When he arrived at his father's palace, Mahomet suddenly kicked his spurs into his horse's side and galloped to the bottom of the steps 'where his brother, a boy of seven years old, was standing to receive him. On meeting, they embraced in a very ceremonious manner, inclining their heads over each other's shoulders. After pipes and coffee, we proceeded to see the apartments; and, as we were walking along, the youngest boy forgot himself a little, and began to skip about; when he was immediately checked by the Pasha, who said: "Brother, recollect you are in the presence of a stranger; walk more quietly." The other instantly obeyed; and it was not a little astonishing to witness such counsel, and so ready a compliance, in children of so tender an age.'

Why was the world no longer as colourful as it was then? Behind my plastic bottles of *Nero* I longed for those times and was dissatisfied with the colourless present. The Turks finally took the town of Its Kale in 1822, after a siege lasting two years. Ali Pasha had conducted himself more and more as an independent ruler, without paying the customary respect to the Sultan, Machmut II. He wisely declined invitations to visit the court – he of all people knew what that would mean. Because, together with his sons Mouctar and Veli, he was gradually conquering the whole of Greece and was, at the same time, upholding independent diplomatic relations with the English, the French and Russians, he had been a thorn in the Sultan's side for many years. The latter finally sent a force of 25,000 men, under the command of Hursit Pasha, to confront him. After all his provocations, Ali had seen this coming. He had already doubled the fortifications in 1815 and, during the siege, he had surrounding parts of the city burned to the ground to leave a clear field of vision for his soldiers to fire.

For a man of 80, he could still put up a good fight. But Hursit Pasha's troops had more endurance and, one moonless night, the tired old man must have left the palace and, together with a few loyal servants and his last love Kyra Vasiliki, climbed into a small boat at the foot of the rocks. They crossed Lake Pamvotis to the island in the dark and hid in the small monastery of St. Panteleimonas.

Not long after the Turks had tracked Ali down and killed him, everything that belonged to the Pasha and could have been identified with him in the future was destroyed. That is why the only Turkish buildings that remain are those for public use, such as the mosque, the bathhouse and the library. And it is why I found myself staring at an empty, sun-baked space, with a bare fake palace on the other side and a grave in which it is said even Ali's headless body no longer rests. If only a small wild animal with rouge on his cheeks would come past, before whom I could prostrate myself on the dusty ground.

I paid and stood up. Tired from so much devastation, I walked back through the gate in the wall, with the intention of leaving the persistent desire for everything that was past behind me. Perhaps I was simply suffering from the same feeling we get when visiting Greek and Roman remains – immense disappointment because our memories seem to let us down. Somewhere in the backs of our minds, in a more primitive part of our brains, there are surely memories of the time when we ourselves walked down from the mountain to the nymphaeum with an amphora on our shoulders?

Where the Bazaar had once stood, souvenirs and rolls of film were now on sale. I bought a better street map than the one I had and spread it out. The vendor looked over my shoulder with interest. He asked me in broken English what I was looking for. I hesitated. Risking that he would consider me insane, I told him I was looking for the house of Niccolo Argyri, where you stayed in 1809.

'Oh, it's on Byron Street,' he replied calmly. 'You will recognise the house immediately, by the plaque.' His index finger moved over the map until it stopped over a small street, not far outside the fortress. I looked at him, amazed. Why should a Greek who sells rolls of film know a Romantic English poet?

'Do you like poetry?' I asked him.

'No, no.' A small cloud passed over his face at the very thought. 'All Greeks know Lord Byron. We learn about him at school in our history lessons. He fought for our freedom. He is a hero, we honour him.'

It will please you to hear this. It is the fulfilment of your ambition: to go down in history as a freedom fighter rather than as a great poet. As I folded up the map, the street vendor laid his hand tenderly on my neck and said amiably: 'If you want to know anything else, just drop by.'


OUTSIDE THE GATE, I was thrust back into the hustle and bustle of the traffic and the crowds of people in the heat. You can have no idea what it is to suddenly step back into my century. Apart from a few old shops selling copperware and shepherds' crooks, you would probably recognise very little. People were eating everywhere, and the restaurants exuded the smell of roast meat. The Greeks I saw as I passed, with their fat bodies and their irritated, weary faces behind plates of charred souvlaki, bore little resemblance to their Apollonian forebears. There was no sign of the noble, mythical people you sought when you left for the birthplace of Homer's epic.

Before I knew it I was standing in Lordou Vironos Street. The street sign hung on the red-painted facade of an old-fashioned textile shop. Through the open door, I looked into the surprised face of the owner, who was sitting doing nothing amidst roles of cloth, some lying on the floor, others propped upright. His raised eyebrows wondered why I was so unusually interested in his business. When I took out my notebook to make a note for myself, the expression on his face turned to that of a victim – I was writing something about him but he would never know what.

Feeling a little fever-struck, I walked on, scouring the fronts of the houses for a plaque. At number three, I came to a halt. Your stay here from 9 to 12 October 1809 was commemorated by an inconspicuous sign, fixed to the peeling plaster of the wall with four rusty nails. But surely this was a mistake. This simple house with light-blue Venetian shutters on the first floor and hideous shop windows on the ground floor looked nothing at all like the villa of Niccolo Argyri that I knew from the engraving. No elegant stairs, no veranda, no pipe-smoker in a fez, no peacock. I didn't take the time to see what was on sale in the shop. Dismayed and insulted, I turned the corner. All this distortion of history was too much for me. Perhaps the villa had once stood on this spot... That was as far as I got in searching for excuses from the Ioannina municipal council, that was probably responsible for the plaque.

Dejected, I walked to the restaurant opposite the city gate and ordered a raki to get over the shock. I had a tzatziki with it, with pale beans the size of a thimble. Why was Argyri's house no longer there? Surely he had not incurred the wrath of the Sultan? Was it burned in 1820, when Ali Pasha's Great Flamethrower spread death and destruction around the fortress? I ordered another raki. That helped. What did I care? Why did I have this continuous feeling of indignation, as though it had all happened only yesterday? After all I don't get all wound up about the fire in the old city hall on Dam Square in Amsterdam which, according to old prints and paintings, must have been a jewel of 15th-century architecture and a lot more people-friendly than the severe Dutch classicist palace that stands there now. There is good reason why biting winds swirl around it as if they want to sweep it away.

Now I could only try and find the Litharitsa palace where Mohamet's little brother had waited for you on the steps. According to my Dutch guide it was on the Platia Dimokratias, near to a clock tower and a park with a belvedere. I crisscrossed the park in all directions and walked around the clock tower three times. An old man who was in the park watching my strange behaviour offered his help.

'Litharitsa...' I said, emphasising every syllable.

He nodded and took me by the hand like a lost child. We started to walk, away from where the palace should have been, and into the main street where the sun was burning down on the house fronts. I looked in amazement at my companion, who was wearing a clean, grey suit of the kind a farmer would put on for a day out in the city.

'Litharitsa,' I repeated.

He nodded reassuringly.

At the baker's, he stopped in front of the window. He pointed temptingly at the cakes and tarts on display and looked at me questioningly. I looked back at him questioningly. Resolutely, he went inside, pulling me with him. At the back he found a quiet corner, with a table and chairs. He sat down in a dignified fashion, adopting the pose of a man of means, and tapped the chair next to him with the flat of his hand, indicating that I should follow his example. But I wanted to go to Litha... Yes, yes, later, he gestured. A piece of cake topped with white powder was placed before me. What else could I do but eat it? Surely I could not turn down his Greek hospitality? The cake was warm and sickly sweet. With difficulty, I managed to eat it, every mouthful observed by two twinkling eyes. He started talking to me animatedly, a cascade of words to which I could only respond vaguely, with a helpless smile. Then he tapped the ring with the blood-coral, that had belonged to my great-grandmother. The young baker's assistant who had served us came to my assistance in broken English.

'He asks if you are married?'

I nodded fervently.

'How many children do you have?'

'Three,' I lied.

So my aged companion was testing the waters for a possible

marriage! That is obviously what women who hang around in parks are looking for, he must have thought. He had put on his best clothes and bought me a cake. Yet this fish would slip through his fingers – but how?

'Will you tell him I am going to take a taxi back to my hotel where my husband is waiting for me?'

The boy translated this faithfully, proud of his knowledge of English. But my admirer pretended not to hear, took my hand and stared at me meaningfully. I pulled my hand away, assured him of my gratitude with a *polí efcharistó* and fled the bakery. He ran after me and while I anxiously tried to find a taxi, he refused to leave my side. I started to walk faster, with the obstinate old codger at my heels – he was very light on his feet for his age.

'*Efcharistó*!' I shouted once more over my shoulder. He grinned roguishly.

A taxi swung into view around the corner. I waved frantically and it stopped. I slid inside and slammed the door. My pursuer had not expected that, and watched crestfallen as I drove off, getting smaller and older. He could have been born in the first Balkan War, when the Greek army put a stop to the Turkish occupation of Ioannina. Did he want to equal Ali Pasha, who still made love to Kyra Vasiliki at the age of 80?

I asked the taxi-driver to take me to the quay, where Daniël was already waiting for me. I boarded the boat, choking back burps of Greek cake. Shortly afterwards we were gliding over the waters of the lake, which seemed greener than ever. Perhaps the water was polluted as punishment for the people it had devoured.

In 1801, Ali Pasha had ordered that 17 young women be drowned in the lake. There are different accounts of the reason for the order. By combining them, I distilled the following details.

One day, Ali found his beloved daughter-in-law in tears. 'What is the matter, my love? Why are you crying?' he asked. Trusting the look in his friendly blue eyes, she confided in him.

'Mouctar no longer loves me,' she sobbed.

'And why not?'

'He gives all his attention to his lover and others that he clearly finds more attractive than me.'

'Then we must do something about that,' said the Vizier resolutely. 'Is there someone in the palace who knows the art of writing?'

She nodded through her tears.

'Have him draw up a list of all the women you suspect and leave the rest to me.'

Like an obedient schoolchild she acquitted herself of her task. She drew up a pretty comprehensive list of the most beautiful women in Ioannina, those who most aroused her paranoid jealousy. At the top, was the name of Mouctar's lover, Frossini, who according to other sources was also Ali's lover, or had been.

There is a melodramatic, postcard-sized painting on sale everywhere in Ioannina depicting the scene. The name of the painter is not mentioned; I assume that he was not there to record the events, like a court photographer. The picture shows only how Frossini is committed to the water. She is sitting in a rowing boat on the lake. A muscular soldier in a uniform ornamented with gold braid, a curved sword like the ones I had seen in the museum at his hip, is lifting Frossini out of the boat, his eyes wide from the effort. It is night. A torch on the bow and a full moon, partially concealed behind wisps of mist, illuminate the scene, which has clearly been depicted with a sense of the gruesome. Ali Pasha himself stands on a rock in the background, his fists clenched, to make sure that his orders are carried out correctly. Frossini's eyes are turned to heaven. Her white wrists and ankles are tied together with rope and a heavy stone hangs from her feet. She is not exactly clothed like a repentant, but is wearing a fine-spun dress, apparently from silk, a finely embroidered smock, and elegant shoes. Her hair blows in the wind. Not for long, you cannot help thinking. In the boat is a second soldier, his gun at his shoulder. He looks at Frossini, his hand open, as if to say: 'How could you have been so stupid?' Next to him, another young woman, one of the 16 that are to follow, hides her face in her hands. In the far distance, more soldiers keep an eye on the events, their guns pointing upwards. It is a poignant glorification of masculine might and collective cowardice towards the utterly defenceless Frossini.

It is said that the women were given something sweet for their last journey. A piece of Turkish delight, perhaps, to enjoy as they gasped for breath? Did Frossini feel guilty in her own way, resigning herself to her fate? Her only guilt was that she had attracted the attentions of the lecherous Mouctar. Under Islamic law, a woman who violated the honour of her family was killed, while the man received no punishment.

The Frossini in the painting should consider herself fortunate that she did not spend her final hours in a closed jute sack. Ali Pasha was not responsible for the punishment of death by drowning for adulterous women. Mostly, the guilty party was thrown into the water in a sack weighed down with stones. Ethel Portnoy, in her book of travel stories *Vluchten*, recalls a Sultan who was so exasperated with his harem that he had all 300 of them thrown into the Bosporus together.

But none of this is new to you. When you lived in Athens, you were returning from Piraeus after swimming one evening, when you encountered a group of riders. They had a sack with them, from which you heard groans. They told you that the Waiwode of Athens had ordered them to cast the sack and its contents, a young Turkish woman, into the sea. You apparently knew her, though no one knows how well. In any case, you went to see the Waiwode in high dudgeon and succeeded in persuading him to spare the girl and send her to Thebes by night.

The incident affected you deeply. '...to describe the feelings of that situation were impossible,' you wrote in your diary. Yet, in your poem *The Giaour*, you made an attempt:

> Oh! Who young Leila's glance could read
> And keep that portion of his creed,
> Which saith that woman is but dust,
> A soulless toy for tyrant's lust?

I looked at the smooth surface of the water. If water can be called a landscape, then Lake Pamvotis was a guilty landscape.

We spent our last day on the island revisiting the final day in the life of Ali Pasha. We climbed the steps to the monastery of St. Panteleimonas, which is built of grey stone, the colour of the mountains reflected in the lake. We bought our entrance tickets on the veranda.

The interior has nothing at all in common with that of a Catholic monastery. The small rooms, with wooden floors and white plastered walls, are furnished Turkish-style, with low red upholstered benches and cushions in Oriental patterns, with a fireplace in the middle. You feel you could easily join the occupants, half lying, half sitting, to daydream by the fire or suck on a hookah. There's nothing I can do about, it looks cosy and inviting, something you would not say easily about the average monastery in Western Europe.

Here, despite being a Mohammedan, Ali Pasha sought sanctuary under the protection of an Orthodox saint. After long negotiations and the pledge of an enormous sum in compensation, he waited for a *firman*, a letter of pardon from the Sultan in Constantinople. It had been promised to him, but Ali would not relax until he held it in his hands. He had agreed with Selim Tsamis, one of his most loyal officers, who he had left behind in Its Kale, that as soon as he received the letter he would send his rosary as a sign that everything was alright. If the rosary did not arrive, Tsamis had orders to set fire to the powder stores so that the entire citadel would go up in flames and the enemy would leave empty-handed.

Ali Pasha did not know that there was a weak spot in his plan – his lover Kyra Vasiliki. On a postcard at least as famous as that of Frossini, she cradles Ali's sleeping head lovingly in her lap, like the Virgin Mary in a Pietà. Kyra felt that his end was nigh. To spare the people of Ioannina the revenge of the Turkish army when they saw their war booty burning before their eyes, she stole Ali's rosary and had it taken secretly to Selim Tsamis at the dead of night. The next day, in the mistaken assumption that peace had been signed, he handed over Ali's provisions and his famous treasure to Hursit Pasha.

The same evening, Hursit's soldiers crossed over to the island. Ali, still waiting anxiously for the *firman*, was unable to sleep. The boat was moored among the reeds and, according to the annals, one Kjose Mechmet Pasha went ashore, followed by Kaphtan-Aga, who had an execution order in his pocket. Half an hour later, they noisily forced entry to the monastery. Ali Pasha sprang out of bed and shouted for them to be calm until he had read the contents of the document.

As he climbed the steps to the veranda, Kjose Mechmet called back that he was bringing the official letter of forgiveness. But Ali did not trust him and ordered his men to open fire. That led to an unsavoury struggle in the cosy little monastery, during which Ali was first shot in the shoulder and then, as Kaphtan-Aga made a clumsy attempt to decapitate him, wounded in the other shoulder. While Ali's soldiers killed Kaphtan-Aga, one of his loyal servants dragged his wounded ruler to another cell, assuming that he would be safe there. But a shot from the cellar below passed through the wooden floor and struck the Lion of Ioannina directly in the heart.

Ali just had time to order Vaïa to kill Vasiliki, who had hidden in a cave during the skirmishes. Was this from love, to spare her rape or worse, or did he – imitating an old Indian tradition – wish her to accompany him to the afterlife? Whatever his motives, Vasiliki was simply handed over to Kjose Mechmet, who treated her with respect as his prisoner.

I scoured the floor in vain for a bullet-hole. The floorboards had apparently been renewed. It is strange to stand on a spot where someone has been killed. It has a kind of perverse quality that you can feel but not see. And the walls, which know everything, reveal nothing. On one of them hangs a reproduction of you, among a mass of prints depicting scenes from the life of Ali Pasha and one of his palaces in Its Kale, still in its full glory. The centrepiece of the collection is a large, kitschy painting showing how the Sultan's soldiers eagerly offer him the head with the white beard.

More appealing, and much more comforting, is a gold-coloured dress worn by a mannequin. It is the dress that Kyra Vasiliki is alleged to have worn on that fateful day.

# Chapter 3

Byron's stay in the Ottoman Empire would last more than two years. Did it change his views on the Greeks and the Turks? He had left England with an ideal image of both, based on childhood fantasies. He had been given a thorough education in Latin and Greek. And had, from a young age, developed a fascination for the Orient. He later said himself: '... all travels, or histories, or books upon the East I could meet with, I had read [...] before I was ten years old.' One of his favourites was Knolles' *Turkish History*, as 'one of the first books that gave me pleasure when a child; and I believe it had much influence on my future wishes to visit the Levant, and gave, perhaps, the oriental colouring which is observed in my poetry.'

During his first journey, he expressed his opinions on both peoples with youthful bravura. He observed them with the noncommittal distance of a passer-by and did not appear to be touched by the less attractive characteristics that he encountered.

'In England, the vices in fashion are whoring & drinking, in Turkey, Sodomy & smoking, we prefer a girl and bottle, they a pipe and pathic,' he wrote merrily. 'I like the Greeks, who are plausible rascals, – with all the Turkish vices, without their courage. However, some are brave, and all are beautiful, very much resembling the busts of Alcibiades; – the women not quite so handsome. I can swear in Turkish, but except one horrible oath, and 'pimp' and 'bread' and 'water' I have got no great vocabulary in that language. They are extremely polite to strangers of any rank, properly protected; and as I have two servants and two soldiers, we get on with great éclat.'

After swimming with them, he expresses his amazement at the following: '... it is a curious thing that the Turks when they bathe wear their lower garments, as your humble servant always doth, but the Greeks not.'

Fourteen years later he left for Greece a second time. Tired of his life in Italy at the side of his lover Theresa Guiccioli, tired of life in general and regularly suffering from attacks of melancholy, he longed for change, for new stimulation that would bring back his vitality and his lust for life. All kinds of wild plans went through his head. On 27 August 1822, he wrote: 'I had, and still have thoughts of South America, but am fluctuating between it and Greece. I should have gone long ago, to one of them, but for infatuation with the Countess Guiccioli; for love, in these days, is little compatible with glory. She would be delighted to go too; but I do not chose to expose her to a long voyage, and a residence in an unsettled country, where I shall probably take a part of some sort.'

'Glory' and 'take a part of some sort' are the keywords here, saying much about his deepest desires: a narcissistic wish to achieve eternal fame among the ranks of heroes, combined with an honest need to help the Greeks in their fight to shake off four centuries of Turkish oppression.

A year later, the decision had been taken. On 22 July 1823, he wrote to Goethe: 'I am returning to Greece to see if I can be of any little use there.' With the support of the Greek Committee in London, he left for the island of Cephalonia, where he waited for several months until the crossing to the mainland would be politically opportune. Waiting for instructions from the Peloponnesus, he started to keep a journal.

His opinion on the Greeks retained none of his earlier bravura. He is pensive, sober and defeatist. If he exaggerates, it is in the negative sense. 'Whoever goes into Greece at present should do it as Mrs Fry went into Newgate – not in the expectation of meeting with any especial indication of existing probity, but in the hope that time and better treatment will reclaim the present burglarious and larcenous tendencies which have followed this General Gaol delivery. – When the limbs of the Greeks are a little less stiff from the shackles of four centuries, they will not march so much "as if they had gyves on their legs". At present the Chains are broken indeed; but the links are still clanking, and the Saturnalia is still too recent to have converted the Slave into a sober Citizen. The worst of them is that (to use a coarse but the only expression that will not fall short of the truth) they are such damned liars; there never was such an incapacity for veracity shown since Eve lived in Paradise.'

Byron can certainly not be accused of being blind to the whims and quirks of the people he had idealised in his youth.

There is no longer any trace of the cheerful absence of obligation of his first journey. He was now completely immersed in the struggle. He staked everything on it: his capital, himself, his life. In Missolonghi, his arrival was anticipated as though he were the Messiah himself, not in the last instance because of the dollars he brought with him. When he finally approached the marshy coast of this inhospitable place, all Greek ships fired a welcome salute.

It was lethal to his élan that, in the months that followed, he was unable to act as a result of squabbling and arguments between the different Greek factions. He wrote to his half-sister Augusta: 'You may suppose that I have something to *think* of at least, for you can have no idea what an intriguing cunning unquiet generation they are, and as emissaries of all parties come to me at present, and I must act impartially, it makes me exclaim, as Julian did at his military exercises, "Oh! Plato, what a task for a Philosopher!"'

FIFTEEN YEARS EARLIER, he did not suspect that his involvement in the Greek tragedy would cost him his life, and in a less than heroic manner. Excited and curious, he and Hobhouse roamed around the northwest of the country, which would remain quietly Turkish and exempt from wars of liberation for the coming 100 years. While the friends were in Ioannina, the Turks celebrated Ramadan by firing pistols into the night at full moon, causing the Greeks to close all their windows and doors – not a melodramatic response when you consider that two bullets landed very close to the house of Niccolo Argyri. Byron and Hobhouse had assumed that Ramadan would be a period of penance and contemplation but, to their amazement, it proved to be a time of excessive feasting that burst forth as soon as the sun had set. After a light meal to satisfy their worst hunger, the Muslims would visit each other. Story-tellers, jugglers, dancers and puppeteers would keep them awake until around one in the morning, when they would dine expansively. They would not retreat to their beds until just before sunrise, where they would stay until around noon. Byron and Hobhouse, kept awake at night by the sound of the drum calling the believers to prayer, found it difficult to plan their journey to Tepelene because there was no one around in the mornings.

The famous painting by Thomas Philips, which was reproduced in *Highroads of English Literature* and invoked in me an infatuated adoration for Byron, would never have existed if, during these days in Ioannina, Byron had not been overwhelmed by the beauty of Albanian weaving and embroidery: 'I have some very "magnifique" Albanian dresses, the only expensive articles in this country. They cost 50 guineas each and have so much gold they would cost in England two hundred.'

In 1814, now long back in England, Byron sat for the portrait. Against the dark background, the Oriental colours – dark red, gold and an almost black dark green – come into their own. His skin has recovered its Anglo-Saxon pallor, his transparent blue eyes look innocently into the world. A scarf is half wrapped around his head in a turban, the loose end hanging quasi-indifferently on one side of his face, covering the small aristocratic ears that so delighted Ali Pasha, and ending in long tassels. The jacket, with all its gold brocade, must have been extremely heavy. He sports a curious moustache, like those officers in love stick to their upper lips in burlesque plays.

If the scene were not so finely painted it could have been a portrait of a medieval knight. The outfit, reminiscent of Lawrence of Arabia, also invokes other associations: the slightly whimsical pose of a film star *avant la lettre*. There is no sign of the misanthropist he was considered to be. Byron himself probably wished to come over as an Albanian fighter, his dagger resting in the crook of his left arm, but I cannot see any soldier going to battle like this. The painting is actually little more than the handsome result of someone in fancy dress. And, in his youth, Byron had once accompanied his mother to a masquerade dressed, of course, as a Turkish boy.

ON 11 OCTOBER, at 1 pm, they left Ioannina heading west. In the meantime, their party had expanded somewhat. Ali Pasha's secretary accompanied them, together with a Greek priest who had not paid the annually required sum in piasters in taxes and wished to explain why to the Pasha in person. Vasilly, who would later play such an important role, also appeared on the scene. He was an Albanian soldier, from the city guard, and had orders to ensure that the Pasha's guests lacked nothing on their journey. The intendant of the post gave them five horses, with a post-man, for the duration of the journey there and back. They were not expected to pay for this service, only to bring a gift for the intendant when they returned.

At first, the journey passed very pleasantly. Hobhouse describes how, after leaving Ioannina, they entered a narrow valley full of orchards and the tents of grape-pickers from the city. A little further, they encountered a house belonging to the Vizier, where part of his harem would sometimes retire. After three hours, they started crossing marshy land. Here, workers were building bridges on the Pasha's orders to keep the area accessible in the winter. At a certain moment, the horse-man galloped off with the horses to find shelter for the night in the next village, Zitsa. The secretary, Vasilly and Hobhouse followed him, leaving Byron behind with the servants and baggage. Around six o'clock, just as complete darkness fell and it began to pour with rain, the leading group made it to village.

They found simple lodgings in the house of the 'Papas', the village priest, and his family. Hobhouse makes no bones about the aversion he felt on entering the primitive room, half-filled with maize, where the smoke from the fire had to escape through the door. When the secretary calmly spread his mat out on the mud floor and sat down on it, he had little choice but to do the same. While Vasilly went to the village to search for eggs and fowl for the evening meal, a storm erupted that made the roof shake. Each flash of lightning was followed by an immediate crash of thunder. At each peal of thunder, the farmer crossed himself, his wife burst into tears, dogs barked everywhere and, in the surrounding mountains, the shepherds bellowed. Hobhouse had never encountered such a storm, and expressed the expectation that he would never experience it again.

He was concerned about what had happened to the others. At 11 o'clock, he gave the order to light fires on the hill above the village and to fire muskets. Shortly after midnight, a deathly pale and totally drenched man collapsed into the room, panting heavily. He started to report to Vasilly, gesticulating wildly. Poor Hobhouse, who understood not a single word, concluded that the whole party had fallen into a ravine. Later, however, it emerged that they had only lost their way and the horses carrying the baggage had fallen. Ten horses and men with torches were immediately sent out to find them.

It was not until three o'clock in the morning that the remainder of the group arrived, and told Hobhouse what had actually happened. Less than five kilometres from Zitsa, they had been overtaken by the storm. They had stopped by some Turkish tombstones that were illuminated by the lightning. There was confusion among the guides about the route – none of them wished to admit that they were hopelessly lost. The dragoman, who had imagined in the midst of the confusion and the apocalyptic weather conditions that they were being attacked by robbers, started to fire his pistol wildly in all directions. This caused everyone to panic. The guides fled and the English servant, Fletcher, began to scream that his final hour had come.

Byron found the entire scene so ludicrous that he burst out laughing. He sat down on a tombstone, protected against the elements by his Albanian cloak, and calmly wrote a few stanzas of *Sweet Florence*.

He later wrote to his mother: 'Fletcher's next epistle will be full of marvels. We were one night lost for nine hours in the mountains in a thunder-storm and since nearly wrecked. In both cases Fletcher was sorely bewildered, from apprehensions of famine and banditti in the first, and drowning in the second instance. – His eyes were a little hurt by the lightning, or crying (I don't know which), but are now recovered.'

You get the impression that Byron enjoyed catastrophes like this, and found them enormously inspiring. From time to time he needed a strong stimulus to feel that he was alive. In *Childe Harolde* he wrote:

Peril he sought not, but ne'er shrank to meet:
The scene was savage, but the scene was new.

Hobhouse saw the incident as proof of the complete unreliability of Greek guides and of servants in general. In emergencies, instead of taking action, they became timid and noisy and wasted all their energy on talking: '... in this country it is absolutely necessary to be always accompanied by a soldier, to enforce obedience.'

The following day they remained in Zitsa to dry their clothes and sort out the baggage. They climbed the hill in the middle of the village, on the top of which – 'like almost every other beautiful spot in these parts of the world' – there was a monastery, dedicated to St. Elias. From the top, they had a magnificent view over hills and valleys, vineyards and flocks of sheep, the Kalamas river winding northwards, and the imposing rocks of Zagorí. Later Byron devoted seven stanzas to an animated description of the natural beauty of this view in *Childe Harold*, including a shepherd, completely in the Romantic spirit.

In the monastery they were received hospitably by a friendly prior. In a comfortable room, he treated them to grapes and a delicious white wine, which the monks had made with hand-pressed grapes. They eagerly accepted the prior's invitation to stay at the monastery on their return from Tepelene.

Yet a curse lay on all this beauty and abundance. Hobhouse had already noted that their host was a little miserable looking. The Papas complained to the secretary, who proved to be a tax inspector in several villages, about the extreme demands that Ali Pasha imposed annually on the people of Zitsa, who were mainly Greek farmers: 13,000 piasters. Almost everything that the rich soil produced – grain, meat, wine, milk, hides – had to be sold, while they themselves and their families suffered from hunger.

Hobhouse was sympathetic to their situation. Not without pathos, he wrote: '... their labour was without reward, their rest without recreation; even the festivities of their church were passed over uncelebrated, for they had neither the spirits nor the means for recreation.' The inhabitants of the archaic village were suffering from collective stress. Ali Pasha no longer had to demean himself by plundering, as he was accumulating enough money through a 'legal' version of it.

Whether the secretary really did put in a good word for the over-burdened villages, the friends were never to find out. As Hobhouse said: '... we never heard how the matter ended.'

# Chapter 4

MY DEAREST BYRON, the island in Lake Pamvotis awoke early, and so did we. As I was packing my rucksack, I realised that I had left my cloth bag on a chair outside the village café the evening before. In the bag was a new Leica that fitted in the palm of my hand. I had bought the camera specially for the journey to Albania, so that there would be no inviting equipment dangling around my neck. Agitated, I hurried back across the cobbles to the square. The bag was gone. The café was shut. I pressed my nose against the window and saw it, hanging in the back in the half darkness, as if it had found itself a safe hiding place. I dismissed all the negative feelings that I had ever had about humanity. Was Rousseau, who you admired so much, right after all? Were people by nature good?

Now all we had to do was wait. A hundred meters away, the boat departed. It came back and departed again. A gaunt woman started to display the contents of her vegetable garden on a wall under a tree: three leaks, five tomatoes, four onions. From the baker's next to the café, the smell of freshly baked bread set our stomach juices flowing, while men and women walked in and out with home-made cakes and pies in flat, round tins, to be baked in the oven. An old man with a rosary between his fingers came strolling up to see if the café was already open. Anachronistically, the village came to life.

Even the fisherman who emptied out a bag full of freshly caught crayfish in the middle of the square seemed to have been resurrected from a time before the lake was polluted. The crayfish, the colour of mud, started to wriggle off in all directions. I jumped backwards. As if they had been given a sign, the villagers emerged from the alleyways to pick the crayfish up by their shells, hold them up to check their quality, and pop them into a plastic bag. With their catches wriggling to escape, they wandered back to their homes. Then the café owner arrived – nodding reassuringly at me from a distance.

THE FIRST STAGE of your journey to Tepelene followed the route from Ioannina to Zitsa. The second finished in the village of Mosure, and the third in Delvinaki. After that you headed for Libohovë, which is now in Albania.

We wanted, as soon as we had crossed the border, to travel as much as possible in the way that was customary in your time. In the correspondence that followed our first meeting, Karagjozi had confirmed our suspicions that the old path across the flanks of Mount Lunxheris was still largely intact. The villages, too, had probably changed little in the intervening 200 years. Making good use of his professorial influence, Afrim Karagjozi made preparations for the journey. How we did not know, but he would make sure that horses – and beds – would be available at the required times.

And, if possible, we would be accompanied by a bodyguard with a moustache that curled up at the ends, and who wore his bullet belt as though it were jewellery. From Paris, where a lot of exiled Albanians live, my son had sent me a warning. He had read in *Le Monde* that, since the arrival of democracy – or what passed as democracy – Albania had become such a wild place that, in the mountains, foreign travellers had been robbed of their baggage and all their clothes by roaming bands of armed bandits in indistinct uniforms – perhaps Ali Pasha's great-great-grandchildren? They were left on the roadside with only what they were born with.

If the paths were still mostly intact on the Albanian side of the border, on the Greek side – where the modern age had had a greater impact and, with no respect for the ancient infrastructure, bulldozers had laid new roads – the original route had largely been covered by asphalt. Daniël seemed to suffer almost physically from all the scars in the landscape. 'Look!' he would suddenly shout in alarm, pointing at a winding road in the distance. 'That wasn't there last year.' We decided to rent the modern equivalent of a team of horses and drive in stages from Ioannina to the point on the Albanian border where you – at a time when everything of course still belonged to Ali Pasha – rode from Delvinaki to Libohovë without any delays. We would try to follow your original route as much as possible and, whenever we came across part of the original path, we would explore it on foot.

We left Ioannina comfortably in a westerly direction, as Hobhouse would say, our rucksacks in the back of the car. We drove along the asphalt road to Zitsa. The marsh described by Hobhouse was drained long ago and turned into farmland. In the hills before Zitsa, where you were overtaken by the storm, military exercises were under way. Perhaps not by coincidence so close to the Albanian border, tanks with long turrets shuffled through the landscape. Sabres and swords, dear George, are now museum pieces, testament to a primitive but picturesque past.

In Zitsa, there is not a single house the same as they must have been in your time. It now has a semi-modern ugliness that you best drive through as soon as possible, going straight on to the top of the mountain, where the monastery of St. Elias still stands.

The wind rustled in the acacias as we stood in front of the gate. Here, you dismounted from your horse. A plaque between moss-covered stones commemorates your visit: 'Lord Byron was here on the night of 12th October 1809'. Underneath is a flattering quotation from *Childe Harold*:

Monastic Zitza! From the shady brow
Thou small but favoured spot of holy ground.

The gate led to you, and to Hobhouse. In this same monastery, you ate grapes, drank wine and conducted, through an interpreter, a laborious conversation with the prior, as is expected of a guest. This is where the journey really started. And even better – the gate was open. We entered through a bell tower, which emphasised our passage into another age, and through a shadowy gateway, we found ourselves in a walled garden.

The monastery stands next to a church dating from 1638. With an almost grim seriousness, an aged gardener was trimming the ivy that grew everywhere. We asked him if we could see the monastery and used your name as a kind of 'Open Sesame'. At first, it was to no avail. It was a blessing that Daniël speaks Greek, and apparently possesses great powers of persuasion – or stubbornness – because he convinced the gardener of the seriousness of our mission. He laid down his shears, climbed onto his moped, and made his bumpy way down the hill to fetch the key.

We said nothing as we strolled through the garden and observed the building from all angles. I climbed onto a pile of rubble in a corner and stared at the entrance.

First I saw the Papas enter the monastery courtyard, followed by the secretary. Then Hobhouse, calm and observant. And finally, you yourself appeared, together with Vasilly, your eyelids slightly swollen from lack of sleep. You handed the reins of your horse to a novice, who tied them to a ring in the wall near the well. The small procession passed under the arches and I saw for the first time how you tried to hide your limp. The prior waited for you in the doorway and, with much ceremony and bowing, you were introduced to him. Could you smell the intoxicating scent of the blooming ivy that covered the walls of the garden? Were the two olive trees already there, and the fig tree in the corner?

It was not easy to bring you to life, and the monastery did not cooperate. It must have been vacated long ago, it looked so introverted and sleepy. At the time of your visit, when it was still in full operation, there were monks walking around, with black anchorite beards and eyes sparkling with religious zeal, as though they had just come down from Mount Athos. They cared for the garden and the animals, received guests and pressed the white, dew-covered grapes with their hands. In the monastery, they prayed, sang, ate, slept and perhaps made love in an unorthodox fashion – I am thinking of the time that you lived in a monastery in Athens and wrestled with the *ragazzi* from the school. Hobhouse says that the monastery did not have to pay taxes to Ali Pasha; can this explain the relative wealth that seemed to surround the prior?

The gardener came back. Without a word, he led us inside; we climbed the stairs to the first floor, where we found ourselves in the refectory. It was a strange feeling for me – for the first time I was standing in a room where you had also been. And who do you think was looking down on the long, narrow dining table from a poster on the wall? There had apparently once been an exhibition commemorating your visit here. In fact, you had effectively replaced St. Elias in such a position of prominence. Once a year, on 20 July – Elias's birthday – life returns to the monastery to mark *Panayiri*. Grain gruel is boiled in large cauldrons. Under your watchful eye, pilgrims sit at the table and, in exchange for a meal, offer small amounts of money for the upkeep of the church and the monastery. And, from the row of ash-trays, it would seem that many of them also enjoyed a smoke after the meal.

We took a look in the bedrooms, furnished with plank beds that denied all definition of whatever has since been devised in respect of comfortable sleeping arrangements. One of the rooms had a stately vaulted ceiling; from the walls archbishops stared at each other into eternity. To me they all looked like Macharios. The most intriguing object was an old wooden board, decorated with wood carving, on which hung a paper list of all the monks who had lived here in the course of the centuries. The ink had faded, the paper had started to peel off, and the edges were eaten away. It had a penetrating smell of damp, the secret destroyer. In this room, too, among the arch-bishops, your memory was honoured. A number of stanzas from *Childe Harold* hung on the wall, next to your portrait. As an arch-sceptic regarding all forms of Christian dogmas, you were in strange company. If the bishops had taken the trouble to open your diaries, they would have been horrified at unorthodox thoughts like: 'It is useless to tell one not to reason but to believe; you might as well tell a man not to wake but sleep.'

'So where did Lord Byron sleep?' I pressed. At every bedroom, I had asked: 'Was it here?' The gardener raised his hands. It pained him to have to tell me, but on the spot where your bed had stood, there was now only a pile of rubble. We followed him, back outside. He pointed to a bricked-up gate high in the bell tower that had provided access to a row of no longer existent cells on the first floor above the stables, running round the courtyard. In the corner where your cell had been there was a pile of stones, half covered with ivy. According to the gardener, it was not even the violence of war that had destroyed the cells, but time, which is much more destructive than man – but in a less conspicuous, more gradual way.

THE PAPAS' HOUSE no longer exists either. Zitsa has been destruc-tively modernised and we were fearful that the same fate had befallen the two other places where you spent the night, Mosure (now Sitaria) and Delvinaki.

It is different in Zagori, the region to the east of the area that you passed through, behind the Mitsikeli mountains. There, Daniël knew, are still a number of villages that, thanks to their remote loca-tion and protective measures by the state, are still relatively unspoilt. Because Megalo-Papingo is one of the oldest of them – dating back to the Byzantine era – we preferred to pass our final nights in Greece there to acquire, paradoxically enough, an impression of how it must have been in Zitsa, Mosure and Delvinaki in 1809.

You would have done the same, if it had been possible in your time. Hobhouse had looked in the direction of Zagori with much fascination, his attention attracted by a spectacular rocky hill 'having a summit so singularly shaped, as to appear like a fortification with battlements and turrets. Papinghi must be part of Zoumerka, and the direct road from Ioannina would lead across it to Nosure; but the mountain being impassable, the traveller is obliged to go fourteen or fifteen miles in a westerly direction to Zitza.' You too must have regretted that you could not travel through these mountains with the allure of the landscapes of Sir Walter Scott.

At the end of the 20th century, you just climb to the top in your rented car, along a road full of hairpin bends. Somewhere halfway round one of these bends, I was so overwhelmed that I forgot to change gear and the car almost ground to a halt. In front of us, on the other side of a gorge that ran close to the road, promising a quick death to the careless, rose a majestic wall of rock. It was a mountain with strata like storeys and a flat top, designed by a Greek Gaudi who, from the earth, had forced up a pantheistic cathedral. Far below, a stream flowed, alternating between azure blue and emerald green. It had cut the deep gorge through the rocks over the course of many centuries.

Megalo-Papingo is the colour of the mountains. The walls, roofs and streets are cut from the rocks, in endless variations of grey. Clouds of silver-grey hops hung over the garden walls. We left the car near the entrance to the village, put on our rucksacks and set off along one of the bumpy tracks past closed, iron-clad gates hiding invisible courtyards. Here, too, they had withstood danger for many centuries. Daniël pointed to the Turkish numbers, nearly rubbed away next to their bright Greek counterparts. The streets were strewn with sheep droppings. Above the village we could hear the tinkling of goats' bells, which made me think of a Tibetan monastery, although I had never been to Tibet.

Behind one of the gates, we found a guesthouse. On the patio, plates of steaming hot *péstrofes*, trout, passed back and forth in front of us. We joined the diners and ordered a bottle of chilled Zitsa wine to celebrate finding the gate of the monastery open and raise our glasses to you and Hobhouse. Today, our journey had really started.

A death's head moth landed between our plates. I pushed my chair backwards. What did this mean? Had it come to warn us? 'Do not enter the land of the Skiptars, or you shall meet with nought but doom and damnation. By all the gods and prophets, I warn you but once.' What would the Oracle of Dodona, not far from Ioannina, have made of this? Surely such a delicate little mechanism, consisting only of a pair of fine-mesh wings, legs and antennae, could not determine our fate? The sign on its back, I told myself, is nothing more than a figure from a Rorschach test: it's all in the eye of the beholder. Suddenly, the moth took off in a zigzag movement – I warn you but once. It would have been good if it had landed on another couple of tables, but no, it disappeared among the vines.

I emptied my glass in one swallow. You would never have allowed yourself to be defeated by a moth with a sign on its back – you loved anything that was a little sinister and had the flavour of a Gothic novel. To put it out of my mind I told Daniël the story of your death's head. One day, the gardener at Newstead Abbey struck a skull with his spade. It had probably belonged to a monk. You were spending Christmas alone at the estate and, in a macabre mood, decided to turn the skull into a cup. For an insane amount of money, you had a jeweller polish it and set it on a silver base, resting on four small balls. As Leslie Marchand describes in his widely praised biography, you did not worry about the bill. It paled into insignificance in comparison with the rest of your debts. The macabre cup passed from hand to hand during drinking sessions with your friends. You wrote a witty poem about it, 'Lines inscribed upon a Cup Formed from a Skull':

Start not – nor deem my spirit fled
In me behold the only skull
From which, unlike a living head
Whatever flows is never dull.

I went for a walk. The sun disappeared behind the mountains, which faded into a misty blue. Around me, the gates squeaked open – widows shuffled outside and sat down on a wall in the cool of the evening. I thought of my mother who now sat alone watching the news, having the miseries of the world pour over her for 20 minutes. I said *kallinigta* and received a chorus of replies.

You will never know, I said to myself, what it is to be a widow, always dressed in black, who has spent her life in an eagle's nest on the – until very recently – inaccessible top of a massive rock and who sits with her fellow widows on a wall under the hops at sunset to wait for bedtime. And to call, with your slightly thinner, but still powerful, voice *kallinigta* to a passing stranger, who cheerfully wishes you a good evening as though she has lived here for years. I would probably not think much of intruders like this, strolling through my village with unashamed curiosity, staring through the cracks in the gates and taking photographs of your 50-times repaired underwear hanging on the washing line.

My bedroom had a Turkish feel, with a low divan bed and hand-woven covers. I hung my clothes over a chair and stepped with one foot into the shower. There was something that looked suspiciously like a scorpion, ten centimetres from my big toe. It *was* a scorpion, a black one with two claws at the front and a sting at the back. It stood ready to attack and I wanted to scream, but thought: no, I don't want to be the sort of woman who needs a strong shoulder to help her at the slightest setback – what's more, I was very naked.

The Fight with the Scorpion – it would make a good book title, I thought. Or perhaps it was one already? I dared not move the lower half of my body. Very slowly, like someone moving against time, I bent my upper body towards the shower head. Carefully I lifted it out of the holder, and pointed it at the insect, away from my feet. Watching the scorpion fearfully the whole time, I turned the tap full on. And then something miraculous happened. As if to help me out of my predicament, the scorpion rolled itself up into a ball, exactly the size of the drain hole. I watched as it slowly circled towards the middle and then disappeared with the water into the drain under the guesthouse. When you think that 90 per cent of all living beings on Earth are insects, each one you rinse away is actually a form of birth control. I kept the shower running for quite some time, because scorpions creep back again while you are asleep and suspecting nothing. After having reproduced themselves in some kind of mysterious way, they come back in their 100s and cross the floor of your bedroom in battle formation to wreak their revenge.

Just before I slept – or was I already asleep? – I saw you lying on a bunk in the monastery of St. Elias. Your face was pale. One arm dangled down while you slept and touched the floor. Ivy started to curl up around the arm and, before I knew it, had covered your chest and then your neck and face. I tried to pull the tendrils, which were affixed with suckers, loose but each shoot I ripped off, grew back just as quickly. The ivy is not real, I told myself, it is just a metaphor.

# Chapter 5

B YRON HAD LONG BEEN FAMILIAR with monasteries. He had inherited one when he was ten years old: Newstead Abbey. Shortly before, his uncle – the fifth Lord Byron, known as the Wicked Lord – had died, so that Byron also inherited the title of Lord. At the time – because of his now dead father's extravagance – he was still living with his mother in great simplicity in rooms in Scotland. It was not until the master at the village school, who was very impressed at Byron's new status, treated him to cake and wine that he realised the significance of his new dignity. When the teacher addressed him by his title in the classroom for the first time, all his classmates stared at him in silence. There was such a sudden distance between him and the others, he burst into tears. He later asked his mother 'whether she perceived any difference in him since he had been made a lord, as he perceived none himself'.

His mother, who had revolutionary ideas and felt sympathy with the common people, was nevertheless proud enough of her aristocratic background to be delighted with the restoration of her status. She decided that she and her 'little Lord' should move to the South and sold most of her furniture to make the journey. Marchand vividly describes the scene that occurred when the coach stopped at the Newstead tollgate.

'Mrs Byron, enjoying the drama of the occasion, asked what nobleman lived on the adjoining state. "It was Lord Byron's, but he is dead," the woman at the gate replied. "And who is the heir now?" the proud mother asked. "They say it's a little boy that lives in Aberdeen." May Gray, later Mrs Byron's maid, exclaimed: "This is him, God bless him!" and turned to kiss the embarrassed young lord.'

Their first impression of the Abbey, which dated from the 12th century and was sold to a distant ancestor by Henry VIII, was overwhelming. Standing together with the ruins of a grey stone Gothic church on the shores of a lake, it was a scene of picturesque charm. But John Hanson, who was waiting for them at the entrance, immediately dampened their joyful enthusiasm by seriously discouraging them from living in this romantic setting. To show them what he meant, he took them to the back of the building, where the roof had long ago collapsed, and the hall and refectory were full of hay for the cattle. He told them that the whole estate, including the farms and the stables, had been heavily neglected and exploited for years to pay off the Wicked Lord's debts. But mother and son would not be dissuaded. They needed take only one look at the gloomy but imposing hall and they were steadfastly determined to live at the Abbey. After a few small repairs were made, they moved in with their few possessions and started to enjoy the country life.

Young Byron was in his element as a large landowner, with a family coat-of-arms – a mermaid with chestnut brown horses – to legitimate his new identity. He found his uncle's old pistols in the abbey and developed a passion for shooting that would stay with him until the end of his life. Three years before the end of his life, he wrote in his diary: 'Rode out, as usual, and fired pistols. Good shooting – broke four common, and rather small, bottles, in four shots, at fourteen paces, with a common pair of pistols and indifferent powder. Almost as good *wafering* or shooting – considering the difference of powder and pistol – as when, in 1809, 1810, 1811, 1812, 1813, 1814, it was my luck to split walking-sticks, wafers, half-crowns, shillings, and even the eye of a walking-stick, at twelve paces, with a single bullet – and all by eye and calculation; for my hand is not steady, and apt to change with the very weather. To the prowess which I here note, Joe Manton and others can bear testimony; – for the former taught, and the latter has seen me do, these feats.'


BYRON WOULD CERTAINLY have felt at home among the Albanians, who loved flaunting their weapons. Since that first shooting practice, he always had pistols with him – which must have been a comforting thought as he travelled through Ali Pasha's lands, a kingdom the latter had accumulated through looting and plundering.

On Friday 13 October, at nine o'clock in the morning, he left Zitsa. Loyal to his task, Hobhouse notes how the journey continued, often resorting to vague descriptions like 'a barren hill' or 'a plain'.

When they reached the Kalamas, which they had seen winding through the landscape from Zitsa, he loses himself in reflections on the true identity of the river. The Secretary claimed it was the Acheron – according to the ancient Greeks, the entrance to the underworld. Hobhouse, seeing no evidence at all that this was the river that flowed into the 'Port of Sweet Waters', suspected that the Secretary's authority was Meletius, a 'modern Greek geographer, who was Archbishop of Athens' in the 18th century. We would not easily call a geographer from a century ago modern. Meletius' book, however, was still a standard work for travellers, despite being full of errors.

When they entered the valley of the Kalamas, they saw a water-fall, 'not very high, but rolling through a grove of trees, with a small mill perched on top of the left bank'. After that, they passed 'woody hillocks' and hills 'covered with trees'. Hobhouse clearly did not make much effort to beautify his use of language. Again, the company was overtaken by a thunderstorm. Around half past one in the afternoon, they arrived, soaked through, at the village of Mosure where the bad weather prevented them from proceeding any further that day. Their stay in Mosure proved to be a repeat of Zitsa. Again they took lodging in the house of a priest, which was even more miserable than the previous one. 'You have seen an Irish cabin,' Hobhouse notes, 'and I need not be more particular.' The whole village belonged to Ali Pasha, as did half of all its produce. His reputation as an excessive tax collector was running ahead of him.

# Chapter 6

My DEAR GEORGE, we drove back from Megalo-Papingo to Zitsa to pick up where we left off. We entered the village from the South, to leave again by the north, with Hobhouse's description in our hands. After a while, the asphalt suddenly stopped. Ahead of us lay a road paved with cobbles, a road to bump along in a coach. This must be how the caravan routes, the Roman roads, the main routes between places of importance looked before roads throughout the world were rolled flat and covered with asphalt, giving them the same grey, lifeless appearance everywhere. The alternative was the goat track, the B-road of the past that used to connect less important villages.

This must have been the road that you used to leave Zitsa, as it was the only one going in this direction. The cobbles were the same – though a little more worn, of course. We parked the car on the side of the road and started to walk. At first we literally followed in your tracks. The surrounding landscape was the same as the one you passed through, and just as remote as it was then. The journey acquired an added intensity, it felt like something in the atmosphere had retained a memory of you, as though in some way or another you were still present in the rocks, trees and plants that we passed. Threatening clouds hung above the mountains, and there was not a breath of wind. Everywhere a subdued silence reigned, making it easier than it would have been in the bright sun to transport yourself back to 1809 and hear the sound of hooves clattering on the cobbles.

I became aware of just how much your journey was one into the unknown as I wandered through this unfamiliar landscape, permeated with my own insignificance. We had the latest maps with us, which were accurate down to the last square millimetre. You had to make do with chaotic maps full of bizarre names, on which the course of a river could easily have been moved a centimetre or so. In the hands of a dragoman, you were on the way to meet an unpredictable stranger, who could make the difference between life and death with a click of his fingers, and about whom you heard very little that inspired confidence as you travelled. Who was to guarantee that you would ever return from Dropull, on the other side of the mountains? In your time, you needed a great deal of courage to make this journey, I realised now, although the tone of your letters was much more one of bravado.

After we had walked for some distance, we returned to the car and drove a few kilometres further. Going downhill, we saw in the distance to the left a Byzantine monastery that Hobhouse did not mention at all. The further we went downwards, the greener the surroundings became (Hobhouse's forests and groves). The robust mountains of the Kassidiaris range looked like sleeping monsters that could at any moment raise themselves up and growl angrily. When we came closer to the Kalamas we parked the car at the side of the road and went farther on foot. In the depths, hidden by a wild tangle of trees and bushes, we could hear the rush of the river. A weathered sign pointed the walker in the direction of a set of crumbling steps. Pushing aside the brambles, we started to descend. We entered a green world of moss, ferns and trees overrun with lianas. Suddenly, below us, we saw the glistening spray of a waterfall as it plunged through a gorge, between large rocks. It was not very high, but wild and effervescent white. The raging water settled into a river that flowed under a stone bridge, carved out of the rocks by the water and strengthened at some time long past with stones. Plants hung from the bridge like lianas.

Halfway, the winding steps emerged onto a small plateau, on which stood the remains of a rotting bench. In better times, to protect walkers, a balustrade had been made of logs nailed together in a criss-cross pattern. It reminded me of sepia photographs of my grandparents, leaning quasi-casually on a similar kind of bridge, but then a fake in a photographer's studio. The whole romantic scene, with steps and benches in late-19th-century style, perhaps once intended for ladies from Ioannina, dressed in corsets and taking a Sunday stroll, must have fallen into disuse and decay long ago. It is remarkable that Hobhouse had so little to say about this spot. I sat for a long time balanced gingerly on a moss-covered rock, my eyes fixed on the mysterious world behind the green curtain of vines. Had

Meletius been right? Could you indeed here, like Persephone, enter the underworld?

We climbed back up, crossed the bridge and descended again on the other side. Hobhouse's grove had become a forest in which, at any moment, Pan could appear, a lecherous grin on his face as he chased a nymph.

After we had sought in vain for 'a small mill perched on top of the left bank', we spent the rest of the day trying to find the bridge that you had crossed half an hour after passing the waterfall. At that point, Hobhouse said, the Kalamas was very rapid and 'in breadth, about the size of the Avon at Bath'. Daniël asked the people of the village of Masariki, which lay farther up the river, but even the village elder knew nothing of such a bridge. From the village, we followed a path to the left of the river, convinced that we were once again on the right route. We had by now become so obsessed with seeking 'signs in the landscape' that my neck was aching. But we were on the right track – in front of us was the plain where you had been caught in the storm.

We nearly suffered the same fate. The sky was heavy with low clouds that seemed ready to burst at any moment. We wouldn't get to Mosure now, as it was already getting dark. We had to be close. Where was the nearest proper road? Surely I wasn't starting to long for asphalt?

Two aged women shuffled past, bent double under a load of maize. We stopped to ask them the way to the 20th century. One of them straightened up jauntily and, with the maize shaking and rustling, explained to us with wide gestures which way we had to go. Following her instructions, just before the water fell out of the sky with full force, we came – via a difficult to follow cart track – to a road that was marked on the map. The rain was so heavy that the windscreen wipers could hardly cope.

On the road along the Vikos Gorge, you could never see farther than the next hairpin bend: 'the torrents, streaming down the hills, had more than once nearly carried away our luggage horses'. Just before Megalo-Papingo, the silhouettes of two people walking lit up on the side of the road. I dared not stop to pick them up for fear of skidding off the road.

A little later, the walkers came into the guesthouse, soaked to the skin. They were a couple from your mother country, of that indeterminate age that you only encounter among the English – perhaps because of their unwrinkled, pale pink skin or their Anglo-Saxon upbringing, which calls for them to remain cheerful under all circumstances. The bus they had taken from Ioannina did not come to Papingo, so they had to walk the last three kilometres, dragging their increasingly heavier Samsonites behind them. Their misery was compounded by the fact that the last Budget car had been hired out – to us! 'Never mind,' they grinned, brushing wisps of wet hair from their faces.

After they had freshened up, they joined us at our table. The landlady lit the wood in the fireplace, while her daughter served up a leg of lamb smelling of thyme. It was the perfect atmosphere to strike up a conversation with your compatriots, who did not seem at all surprised that we were following in your footsteps. They lived ten kilometres from Newstead Abbey, but had never been there. They did tell us, however, that your grave had been badly neglected.

'Quite a fool, Lord Byron,' opined my table companion.

'An extraordinary man,' I said.

He held his hands up in resignation, after all you didn't contradict a lady you didn't know. Had your image not changed in two centuries? 'You may easily suppose that the English don't seek me, and I avoid them,' you wrote with good reason from Venice in 1817.

THE FOLLOWING MORNING, the only reminder of all the water that had fallen from the heavens was a slowly rising mist. The autumn sun broke through in long rays of hazy light. Today we had to reconstruct your journey from Mosure to Delvinaki and find the place where you crossed into Albania. The following day, Professor Karagjozi would meet us at the present-day official border post, some five kilometres farther to the south.

We drove directly to Mosure. The only thing there that dated from your time was a thick oak on the village square, with an imposing leaf canopy. The rest was... well, it is becoming monotonous to describe variations in ugliness. Many of the houses, Daniël thought, were built by guest workers returning from America or Germany. The explanation brought little relief. The encounter with a different culture had produced a building style without identity, neither Greek, nor American or German. We wandered around, uninspired. Near the oak, there was a monument to those who fell in 1912. It had taken a century for the farmers here to rise up against the feudal Ottoman regime. 'Here also we saw a house belonging to the Vizier,' wrote Hobhouse. 'Indeed the village itself, they told us, was his private property.'

An ancient Toyota van bounced past, packed solid with villagers, leaving behind a dull silence, the silence of a village where nothing ever happened.

On Saturday 14 October, you left the village in a northerly direction, passing through thick forests of oak, with the Kalamas to your right. We did the same, slowly, as a lorry full of timber trundled along in front of us. In your time, the wood was transported by river: 'The villagers [...] were employed in felling timber in the mountains, which, after being cut into planks, is passed down the Calamas to the coast.' Halfway we noticed that the road curved too far to the west. We turned round and stared into the undergrowth until it nearly gave us headaches in search of a trace of the original path.

For the umpteenth time, we consulted Hobhouse: '... in a little more than an hour [we] skirted a small plain and lake, also the right.' The lake was on our map. On the north side, the road to the Albanian border passed along its edge. Making a wide curve, we drove to the spot where the two almost touched, parked the car and walked along a sandy path that headed into the country to the south of the lake. That led to a small road that, as Hobhouse described, ran along the west side of the lake. But where did it come from? We followed it back in the direction of Mosure and stumbled on a sunken path between the oaks that later crossed a small plain. At last. The oak forests, the plain, the road to the lake on the right side – they were all still there, though it would seem no one ever came here. Every time we found the original path, I was struck by a light euphoria. It was the reward for searching on the basis of notes made nearly two centuries before, and I was whisked unexpectedly back through time. With a little effort, we could see the whole caravan come past, Hobhouse at the front, craning his neck to see everything and scribbling fervently in his notebook. We joined the company as simple foot travellers, walking along behind in the clouds of dust thrown up by your horses, and saw what you saw. Toadstools in the verge, rosehips, wild plums, a field full of autumn crocuses, sheep droppings on the path and, everywhere, birds that with great spectacle took their fill of the abundance of fruits. Did you stop on the banks of the lake and stare at the smooth surface of the water, in which the flattened mountains were reflected? Did you feel like taking a swim, or was this overgrown pond insufficient challenge for you, accustomed as you were to crossing sea straits?

After the lake the path curved too far to the left and we lost the trail again. We walked back to the car and followed the signs to Delvinaki. The more the road crawled upwards, the deeper the precipice to the left became. Behind the orange-red cotinus shrubs along the side of the road we got an increasingly clear view of the massive, rolling mountains on the other side. 'Albania,' said Daniël. It sounded like a threat.

Still climbing, we reached a point where our road intersected the old path. From the gorge, it crossed the highway exactly at the crown of a bend. We left the car on the only flat space we could find and descended into the gorge until, at the bottom, we found a well-preserved stretch of an ancient paved road and a small arched bridge. A bunch of wild cyclamen shone purple under the arch. Entranced, we lingered near this remnant of a long-gone network of roads, perhaps from Roman times, a lost relic in the landscape. I had an attack of nostalgia for a way of travelling that was bound up with beauty: the roads, bridges, inns, coaches, horses and pack animals, even accessories like trunks and baskets, somehow completed the landscape. No wonder they were so frequently portrayed in prints and paintings.

We wondered how you manoeuvred a horse across such a narrow bridge. Would we be able to do that later, in Albania? Suddenly agitated, we turned about and headed in the direction you had taken. Where the path turned, you had turned, and I turned with you. Where you had climbed, I climbed. Hobhouse complains of 'large masses of loose rock'. Under our feet, stones, earth and rubble rolled down the slope. 'Here the path is concealed under two centuries of erosion,' said Daniël, in a schoolmasterly voice.

When we reached the top we saw Delvinaki below us in the distance. 'Here we were more comfortably lodged,' Hobhouse was pleased to report. '[It] is, on the whole, a clean town, containing [...] three hundred habitations, peopled by Greeks. Of these, the greater part are employed in cultivating the ground, or in attending their flocks on the neighbouring hills; but a few of them style themselves merchants, as they bring small wares on horseback from Constantinople, Salonica, and Ioannina, and sell them in the inland towns of Albania and Roumelia. These merchants are necessarily absent from their own houses the greater part of the year.' Ali Pasha ordered that the wives and children of the merchants be detained at home, to ensure that his subjects returned.

The villagers told you that the Pasha had spent three days in the 'town' a week previously. You were getting warm! They thought he was now most probably in Libohovë, your (and our) destination for the following day. Hobhouse still had the energy for an evening ramble after 'the fowls, eggs, and grapes, which always composed our meal.' He climbed a slope and enjoyed 'a prospect on every side magnificent' and 'the last rays of the setting sun' – something that would never have flowed from your pen.

Delvinaki is still an orderly village. The Orthodox church – contrary to the tradition of the region – has been plastered and whitewashed, too clean and bright for a house of God. Even the spring is a century too young in its current form, according to Daniël, who discovered that it dated from 1908.

We had difficulty finding the right route in the direction of the Albanian border. '...in order to regain our road, [we] were obliged to ascend and descend a steep zigzag stony path.' That didn't help us much, no matter where you went here, you had to ascend and descend. Because time was getting short we asked the way from a woman in a striped apron, who was lighting an oil lamp in a small chapel just outside the village. She asked us for a light and I rummaged around in vain in my bag for the lighter that had lain in the bottom for years, together with a penknife and a few other bits and pieces, just in case 'I got lost in the forest'. With an unfathomable smile, she pointed to the north: we were on the right road, but we could not enter Albania this way. We knew that. We waved to her and drove on. The woman was observing an old tradition: lighting a candle or lamp every evening in one of the small chapels alongside the road – some no bigger than a shoebox on a stick – which have served as beacons for travellers for many centuries. At the spot where Hobhouse noted the 'broken remains of a bridge', we crossed the Drino. The river would get to Tepelene before us – we had to go through the mountains. We took a chance and turned left towards Pontikátes. The road climbed slowly and, at a junction, revealed an unexpected panorama. Two small chapels with plate glass and a lonely cypress, with one branch lashing anarchically out of line, seemed to urge the traveller to rest for a moment and take in the landscape he was about to enter. Far below us lay the marsh of Xerovaltos, drained by Ali Pasha and now covered with fields and grazing sheep.

We descended through a forest and crossed the former marsh until the road became a sandy path. We could see that it headed directly between two mountains to the Albanian plain of Dropull.

There could be no doubt: you and Hobhouse had passed this way. Feeling safe in the car, we drove on into the border country about which we had heard such wild tales. Imagine that this humble little path had escaped the notice of the border guards. I would love to have made that single symbolic step across the border – at exactly the same spot where you, little suspecting that it would be impossible in the political configuration of two centuries later, simply trotted along on your horses.

We came to a sign that declared implacably that we had reached a military zone. We stopped, a little startled, and stared full of longing along the innocent-looking path, where the blackberries lining the edges were certainly no sourer than those outside the forbidden area. We didn't dare to get out of the car, imagining bullets from the undergrowth flying about our ears. It was a difficult moment, as I sat there gnashing my teeth. We were so close. It was bizarre, and somehow unfair, not to be able to go any further. Just like you not being able to travel via Gjirokastër because the town was in the hands of the enemy, Ibrahim Pasha, we could not go any further here because of a clash of competing spheres of power. After your journey, the borders in Europe shifted considerably for some time. They have only been relatively stable – like those in the rest of the world, as a matter of fact – for the past half a century or so. Conquering countries no longer pays off, except in the Balkans where, as the result of old-fashioned violent conflicts, new borders have been drawn.

We drove back into Ali's marsh, silent and, for the moment, robbed of our enthusiasm. I immediately regretted that we hadn't driven on – I was just a scaredy-cat. They were right; I couldn't throw knives. Near an old barn, the only building on the plain, we turned left on a whim. Perhaps we could see how your route continued further from the mountains on the other side of the plain.

The road, which was strewn with sharp stones, climbed steeply. I prayed silently that we would not breakdown here, so close to sunset. We had chosen a perilous time to make this trip. We drove through the narrow streets of a village high up on the mountainside, where two priests with impressive bellies were just shuffling out of their sanctum, smacking their lips as though the Corpus Christi had tasted especially good today. We bumped our way higher and higher until the road reached a dead end in a hamlet where four young soldiers in camouflage trousers and T-shirts sat yawning and scratching their heads. Curious, they came over to us. Daniël told them about the strange purpose of our journey. Lord Byron? They nodded vaguely. Perhaps their own mission, capturing Albanians who crossed the border illegally, was so alienating that everything else just paled into insignificance. Apparently, only a moving dot in the landscape could rouse them from their lethargy. We took our leave of them in comradely fashion, falsely creating the impression that we were naturally on their side. We Europeans united against the Albanian barbarians, who shouldn't think they can just come here and benefit from all our achievements after they turned their backs on us for so many decades in arrogant silence.

Behind the soldiers' backs, I could see that the road continued in an even more primitive form in the direction of the border. We turned around and started to descend until, unexpectedly, on the other side of the valley, we saw the now forbidden path into Albania. We could see that, on the Albanian side, the slopes were rust-brown as the result of a forest fire.

We could see you and your companions, transparent as a procession of spectres should be. You and Hobhouse at the front galloping across the grass-covered plain. The figure at the back, slumped exhausted on his horse and appearing to suffer the journey in silence, must be poor, persecuted Fletcher. You could hear him groaning from far off. Our eyes followed the slowly moving column, a ribbon of ants, until the rapidly setting sun cast its shadow over you and you disappeared from sight.

We had to hurry to get home before dark – the hairpin bends of Papingo were waiting for us.


BACK AT THE GUESTHOUSE, a group of German hikers had arrived who were aiming to climb to Drakolimni Lake in the Tymfi mountain range and then to descend into the Vikos Gorge.

'That's not something you'd be likely to see the Greeks doing,' said Daniël. 'They don't care about nature at all. They come to Papingo out of snobbery, stroll through the village for a while, take a quick indifferent look at the gorge and then take refuge in a restaurant.'

He was prompted to make this remark by the Greek families around us, who occupied the remaining tables and were eating with relish. Their shoes suggested that they never planned to set foot in the mountains.

'That is not just typical of the Greeks,' I said. 'The people of the

Mediterranean do not walk. At most, they take a stroll in the park, or along the boulevard in the evening.'

Next to us was a large American of Greek origin who solemnly declared that he intended to descend into the Grand Canyon of Epirus. The fact that he was born in the country of unlimited opportunity was too strong for his genes. He filled our glasses to the brim with retsina. I did not have the courage to refuse, though I shared Hobhouse's aversion: 'The Greeks consider that the resin gives the strength which the water takes away, and that the lime refines the liquor, but it is to this process that a very unpalatable harshness, generally to be met with in Greek wine, is to be attributed.'

Our table companion had been a professor of economics at the University of Athens for a number of years. He had not come to Greece to seek his roots, but out of curiosity. That had since been relatively well satisfied and he had concluded that he was more American than Greek. 'This country will never come to anything,' he said animatedly, taking a large gulp of wine. 'What have they done with the money from the European Community? Nothing. Look at the industry, the ports – it's enough to make you cry. They'll never compete with the West. And the worse they do, the more nationalist they get. And all that boasting about their ancient forefathers. But I like it here,' he grinned. 'I'll hang around for a while.'

We started to talk about the ancient Greeks. It was doubtful whether the modern Greeks descended from them, given the mishmash of ethnic groups that had settled on Greek territory in the past 20 centuries. And then there was the major exodus of Greeks during the era of Turkish domination. Were the ancient Greeks blond? Were the Gods blond? On this controversial theory, after the glasses of retsina had been cleared from the table and replaced by the much smaller glasses for raki, we let our imaginations run increasingly freely.

How we got from blonde gods to brown bears, I don't remember. I think the hikers on the next table had wondered aloud what they should do if they came across a bear on their path.

'Nothing,' Daniël said. 'A bear won't hurt you either.'

They had touched a nerve. In one of his travel guides, under the heading 'A bears' friend in Kipi', he had devoted a great deal of attention to the seriously depleted bear population in the Pindus mountains. The 'bears' friend', Yorgos Mertzanis, was a biologist who had been living in Kipi for many years conducting research into the brown bear for his PhD. For Greek hunters, the bear is a favourite trophy that he believes shows his *andrismós*, his masculinity. Farmers and herders still see the bears as a threat and see this as a justification for killing them under the pretext that the animals had attacked them. The forest fires and radical changes in the landscape do the rest. An electricity company, for example, had threatened to turn the Bear Stream into a reservoir.

In Western Europe, the brown bear still exists only as an animal in fables – the oafish Bruno against the clever Reynard the fox – and as a cuddly toy in dungarees and a floppy hat. Even in the woods, there is more chance of you meeting a teddy-bear than a real bear of flesh and blood. Since we only know bears as infantilised imitation animals, the thought of meeting a real one makes us shudder.

Daniël gave the group some good advice to take with them. 'If you encounter a bear that is standing up, do not be afraid. He is short-sighted, and you are just as unusual a sight to him as he is to you.'

# Chapter 7

As a student in Cambridge, Byron bought a tame bear. He kept it in a small hexagonal tower above his rooms. He wrote to a female friend: 'I have got a new friend, the finest in the world, a tame bear. When I brought him here, they asked me what I meant to do with him, and my reply was, "he should sit for a fellowship".' It was not normal to keep a bear and Byron enjoyed the sensation he caused when he took his unusual pet for walks on a chain.

At that time, he also had a Newfoundland, Boatswain, a loyal companion whenever he was at Newstead Abbey. But the dog contracted rabies and died in front of Byron's eyes. Byron, who had no idea what was wrong with the animal, continued to wipe the slaver from its lips as it succumbed to the paroxysms. He was stunned by Boatswain's sudden death. The beloved dog was buried in the garden and honoured posthumously with an epitaph in verse.

Byron surrounded himself with animals for his entire life. Ten years after this journey through Albania, when he was living in the Palazzo Mocenigo in Venice, he accumulated a colourful menagerie of four horses, two monkeys, a fox and two bull mastiffs. The mastiffs had been sent by his publisher, John Murray. Byron wrote to him: 'The Bulldogs will be very agreeable – I have only those of this country who though good – and ready to fly at any thing – yet have not the tenacity of tooth and Stoicism in endurance of my canine fellow citizens: then pray send them by the readiest conveyance – perhaps best by Sea.'

Byron also collected servants as though they were pets. In Venice, he had 14. The remarkable Tita, who he had originally employed as a gondolier and whose frightening demeanour and wild beard commanded respect from everyone, served his master with the loyalty of a dog.

He was attracted by the animal element in women and boys, too. About a Venetian lover 'with eyes flashing, and her dark hair streaming in the moonlight', he says: 'I like this kind of animal'. Yet, after his divorce from Annabella Millbanke ('my mathematical Medea'), he refers to her as a 'cold-blooded animal'.

RIDING BETWEEN TWO MOUNTAINS, the friends entered the country that is now known as Albania, 'until in three hours from Delvinaki, we came at once upon a very wide and long plain, running from south to north, well cultivated, divided by rails and low hedges, and having a river flowing through it to the south. On each side of this plain was a ridge of barren hills, but covered at no great intervals [...] with towns and villages, which appeared, like the goats of Virgil, to hang upon the rocks. These, we were told, were in the district of a large city called Argyrocastro, which we saw indistinctly at a great distance, as we advanced to the north along the side of the hills, that form, as it were, the eastern bank of this extensive plain.'

The invisible wall that now runs through old Epirus and the former territory of Ali Pasha dates from 1913. Between 1910 and 1912, there were a number of uprisings against the Turks in Albania, which brought to an end five centuries of occupation. The victory was sealed with the declaration of the independent democratic state of Albania. Until the last minute, the surrounding states had tried to divide the territory of Albania up amongst themselves, denying the existence of an Albanian people with its own language. In 1913, an international commission was established in London to monitor developments in Albania and to set definitive borders – and the gentlemen sitting around the table promptly cut the size of the country by half. South Epirus went to Greece and Kosovo to Serbia, a decision that continues to have fateful consequences today as that same international community tries to restrain a conflict created around that same table.

Since then a line – dash-dot-dash – crosses the map of the region, even proving watertight in the strait between Corfu and Albania. Here and there it cuts right through population groups that have the same origins and have traditionally shared the same language and religion. A census in the same year showed that there was a small majority of Greeks living in South Albania, a fact that is still used by extreme nationalists who want to see the region annexed to Greece.

The small majority themselves are less fanatical, demanding only the freedom to preserve their own language and culture, also in their own schools.

It was in this border region that Hobhouse observed the first Albanians: 'The dress of the peasants was now changed from the loose woollen brogues of the Greeks, to the cotton kamisa, or kilt of the Albanians, and in saluting Vasilly they no longer spoke Greek. Indeed it should be mentioned, that a notion prevails amongst the people of the country, that Albania, properly so called, or at least the native country of the Albanians, begins from the town of Delvinaki; but never being able, as I have before hinted, to learn where the line of boundary is to be traced, I shall content myself with noticing the distinction in the above cursory manner.'

If the border was imaginary then, it is now as good as impenetrable. Every day, Albanians – in groups or alone – try to cross it in search of work. Some of them are young boys no older than 15. Greek soldiers – like the ones we encountered in their remote post high in the mountains – have the job of tracking down and rounding up these desperados. It is like a computer game. When they have gathered enough Albanians, they put them in a bus and take them back to the official border crossing, where they are deposited back in their reservation.

The Albanians then disappear immediately into the mountains to try again.

# Chapter 8

M Y DEAREST FRIEND, in the bus on the way to the border, I saw my first Albanians. They were more finely built than the Greeks. I also imagined I saw a more fiery look in their eyes – like that of the double-headed eagle on their flag. On the Greek side, the road was being renovated, perhaps with a view to the improved trade relations with Albania since there too an embryonic free-market economy has started to develop.

Just before the border, we passed rows of second-hand trucks, bought by Albanians in Germany, England or the Netherlands. We got out of the car and settled in for a long wait. With our rucksacks, we stood out among all the Albanians returning home – there were no tourists to be seen. Daniël in particular, with his shepherd's crook, was the subject of much curiosity. On the other side of the trellised fence, taxi drivers loudly tried to attract our attention.

The Greeks let us jump the queue and allowed us through. On the Albanian side we were taken to a small office by the most spectacular customs officer I have ever seen: a raven-haired beauty in a tight-fitting denim suit and high heels, with a revolver in her belt. Inside, our passports were studied with a frown. We mentioned the name of the professor who was waiting for us, but to no avail. What now? As we stood there in awkward silence, the door opened and two police officers came into the office. Were we here to meet Professor Karag-jozi? We nodded, dumbfounded. Suddenly, everything was in order, we were given our passports back and led across a flat, sandy patch of land, picking our way through a confusion of randomly parked Mercedes cars, probably stolen in Western Europe.

There, from a car, the small man emerged who I had last seen in the half-light of a station restaurant. Our cordial greeting was full of relief – the journey we were about to make was so unusual that both of us had secretly doubted right up to the last minute whether it would actually happen.

The first cloud passed over the face of Afrim Karagjozi. The man with the horses, who should have been there at 11 o'clock, was nowhere to be seen. It was now midday. Because there was not even the simplest of places to find refreshment at the border post, the officers suggested that we go for a cup of coffee in a nearby village to make the wait shorter. Everyone there was very friendly. We learned our first words of Albanian: *faleminderit* (thank you) and *mirupafshim* (see you). They laughed at our clumsy attempts, and we laughed because the language sounded like a parody of itself. Karagjozi was at least as excited as we were. For the first time he could travel around freely in the area in which he was born.

We returned to the border, but there was still no sign of the horses. The police officers suggested driving to meet the horse-man along the old path they assumed he would be taking. We eagerly agreed – it was frustrating that we couldn't finally start our long-awaited journey.

The heavily laden, dilapidated Mercedes bumped over cobbles and potholes, creaking with indignation. As we emerged from one particularly deep hole, the exhaust pipe broke. To make things easier, it was removed and we continued the journey until the path became too difficult even for the seasoned old Mercedes. We got out, and our rucksacks were unloaded, together with the professor's conspicuously small travel bag. We waited, leaning on an old stone bridge, becoming increasingly restless inside without admitting openly that such a start was putting a damper on our enthusiasm. Squinting, we looked across the surrounding plain for the horse-man, who had left us so woefully to our fate. The professor, who was more and more obviously trying to contain his anger, passed around a packet of Albanian biscuits that tasted of nothing and just increased the general feeling of lethargy. One of the policemen, who in all innocence bore the name of the epic poem *Ilyás*, suggested continuing on foot to the nearest village on our route, Peshkepi. He knew the area like the back of his hand and could accompany us as a guide, while his colleague drove to the village over passable roads, with our baggage in the back, and met us there.

Although it was not at all in your style to enter Albania on foot, one look at the mountains to the east, through which we would have to walk and where it would be dark by seven o'clock, was enough to make us realise that we had little choice.

The enormous plain that we crossed had been created by the Drino bursting its banks. Until recently, this part of the valley had been a strictly forbidden military zone. In his paranoid fear of foreign invaders, Enver Hoxha, president and absolute ruler of Albania for some 40 years, had ordered dome-shaped concrete bunkers, accommodating one or two snipers, to be built at strategic locations throughout the country. Every Albanian should have their own little bunker, that was the motto. Feeling slightly alienated, we walked between these crazy-looking buildings, the products of a sick mind, and absurd in a nuclear age. It was warm and hazy. We crossed the shallow river that flowed over a bed of white gravel. With soaking wet shoes, I walked on, wondering why Hobhouse decided to have the river flowing south, instead of to the north where, just before Tepelene, it joined the river Vjosa.

We left Hoxha's shooting range behind us and came to a more pleasant region full of small fields. A farmer and his wife were picking silverskin onions barefoot, watched by a grandmother in a decoratively knotted Arabian headscarf, sitting at the foot of a tree. A curious and amused look appeared on all their faces at the strange sight of our motley company, on a road on which no strangers had been seen for perhaps half a century.

The landscape became more hilly. Ilyás picked wild pears and gave them to me to taste. We gradually came closer to the point between the two mountains where you and Hobhouse would make an appearance. The burned forest on the slope that we had seen to the west the evening before from the Greek mountains, now lay to our east. We kept climbing until we came to a wider path, paved with stones and still as intact as the Via Egnatia, pictured in the travel guide, which runs elsewhere through Albania and once served as a commercial route between Rome and Constantinople.

'This is the road,' said Daniël laconically. All four of us stopped and followed the road with our eyes as it, calm as you like, entered Albania from Greece. For centuries, it had been a through-route for travellers to and from the south, but now it was a dead end, because of decisions made at the beginning of the century by a bunch of interfering diplomats who were by now long dead. While the others continued, I walked the other way a short distance, to meet you. The path moved me, it was so abandoned and useless. But that was an illusion – you could appear round a bend at any moment.

It was a pity that your path did not pass through the region where, for centuries, people lived by the Canon. There, where the Albanian mountains became practically impassable, lived the Malësori, the only people who successfully opposed the Turks, who had in vain tried to incorporate the unassailable mountains into their empire.

While the rest of Albania had been ruled for five centuries from Constantinople, the Malësori obeyed only their own law, the Canon. It had been introduced by Lek Dukagjini, a ruler from the north of the country, who had helped fight the Turks during the expansion of the Ottoman Empire in the 15th century. Since then, social life in the mountains had been completely subjected to the laws and rules of the Canon, which regulated everything relating to marriage and inheritance, property and theft, the position of women, adultery, murder and manslaughter, and the rules of hospitality, without the intervention of a single notary, lawyer or judge. Decisions relating to the law were taken by a Council of Elders, consisting of the oldest and most respected male members of a clan. At the core of the Canon was the honour of the family, the clan, the tribe. Blood feud, vendetta, was the main instrument for restoring lost family honour – the cause of which could be a simple argument between neighbours over a piece of land, an adulterous woman, or an insult which could offend an entire tribe. Children learned from a very young age that they had to weigh up every word before speaking. Vendetta was subject to very strict conditions and was restricted to the men. A man was obliged, whether he wanted it or not, to commit an honour killing if the honour of his family had been violated. As most men sooner or later became involved in an honour-related issue, even if they were not guilty of any form of misconduct at all, there were few men who died a natural death – in fact, it was almost a scandal if they did. Whenever a son was born, they would express the wish that he 'may not die in his bed'.

When Albania became independent, the new government and the church tried in vain to put a stop to blood feuds. Communism, which penetrated every remote corner of the country, succeeded – although, across the northern border in Kosovo, the practice apparently survived for a long time. But if there is such a thing as a communal soul, a rudiment of this tradition continues to be part of the Albanian soul, and it remains advisable to watch your words. 'A head for a head' is not a pleasant prospect.

As travellers, we would have been in a privileged position. The law of hospitality laid down in the Canon would have applied to us. The guest was sacred, and had to be given every comfort, as though the house were his own. The host should even give up his bed, if necessary. And anyone who had a guest in their home was, at that moment, exempt from a blood feud. A guest thus compelled conflicting parties to accept a cease-fire, a role I would have liked to play myself!

We were now walking along the side of the mountain in a northerly direction, parallel to the elongated valley. The first Albanian we met on your path was a sprightly old man, who was riding a donkey side-saddle. He had sticks with him and a rope, but the Lord knows what he was going to do with them. We stopped to exchange our personal details, which I soon discovered was customary when people meet. *Mirë dita*, good day, where have you come from and where are you going? Once we knew everything about each other, he broke into a wide smile, showing three teeth, and wished us *udhë e umbarë*, a pleasant journey.

We passed a small Byzantine chapel, surrounded by cypresses. It must have been overlooked, hidden here in the periphery of Enver Hoxha's utopia, during the great programme of purification. In the 1970s, Hoxha gave orders for all churches and mosques to be demolished or given a non-religious purpose – the only god that the people were permitted to worship was he himself. We walked around the chapel and touched it, struck by the desolation around it. Tenth century, announced a stone above the door. With the stubbornness of nature, Parthenocissus was persistently carrying out Hoxha's orders.

'Can you see that?' Ilyás pointed to a rock high above the path. We could see the vague contours of a building. A few years ago, he told us, a small group of Albanian soldiers who were guarding the border had been murdered by Greeks. The killers had never been caught; perhaps they were extremists or fervent supporters of a reunited Epirus. Again, I thought of the young Greek soldiers sitting out their time in the remote post in the mountains. Their Albanian counterparts had probably been just as bored, waiting for their replacements to relieve them, never suspecting that they were about to be relieved by eternity.

'By the way,' I asked Karagjozi. 'Why weren't you in Athens for the Byron conference? I missed you there.'

The professor snorted with laughter.

'Because I wasn't invited. Without an official invitation from the Greek Byron Society, I couldn't get a visa.'

It turned out he had exchanged letters on the matter with Professor Raïzis, who had argued that it was impossible to invite an Albanian because of the tense relations between Greece and Albania. He had accused the Albanians not only of seeking the support of the Turks, but also of being pro-Turkish for many centuries. He recalled that, in 1821, at the time of the Greek struggle for independence, a large part of the Turkish army had consisted of Albanians.

'But that's ridiculous,' I said. 'Bringing up such an old affair like that.'

Daniël grinned. He knew the Greeks. The professor sighed.

'I tried everything, but his mind was made up.'

'So typical of the Balkans,' Daniël concluded. 'The enemy of my enemy is my friend, that's the motto here. The Albanians are anti-Serb because of Kosovo, so the Greeks are pro-Serb.'

'What a complicated situation,' I exclaimed.

'There are no simple solutions for this region,' he said philosophically.

We arrived in Peshkepi, a cluster of farmhouses, many of which were empty. Outside the only bar, at a small table under a tree, Ilyás's colleague sat waiting for us, his moustache glistening. The meeting was cordial, as though we had known each other for years. Beer was served – Amstel. I had travelled all the way to the hinterland of Albania to drink Dutch beer! I put the white grapes on the table that I had bought in Greece, and Karagjozi passed the biscuits around again. Someone came with small, dark-blue grapes, another added walnuts and pomegranates to the still life on the table. New chairs were fetched, villagers joined us at the table and, before I knew it, they all seemed to be talking at the same time. Karagjozi made a sterling effort to translate everything. Amazingly, everyone seemed to know that you had once passed this way. Perhaps by word of mouth? They found it very amusing that we were following your tracks and we were fortunate that the professor's presence gave our mission a scientific tint.

'At one o'clock we came to a village where there was a bar. Here we stopped, and as we were seated on our mats taking some refreshment, an Albanian handed round several specimens of snuff, for in this village, they informed us, there is the most extensive snuff manufactory of any in European Turkey.'

Snuff has long been replaced by the cigarette – everyone around me was smoking like there was no tomorrow. Someone showed me an ingenious way of opening walnuts with a pocket knife, another how to eat pomegranates without having to fight with the pips. Because I was alone in male company in a region where the sexes traditionally live separately, the landlady threw her arm around my shoulders sympathetically. Then, laughing, she pinched me in the biceps to see if I were man enough to actually complete the journey that was such a source of amusement to all and sundry.

And still there was no sign of the horse-man. Some of the villagers told us that he had been seen around 10.30 that morning in Libohovë. 'Then,' said Ilyás, 'it would be impossible for him to be at the border at 11 o'clock.'

The sun was already casting long shadows when we got into the Mercedes that would take us back, via a road through the valley, into the mountains to Libohovë, the largest village on our route. Like you, we had planned to spend the night there. In the car, Karagjozi's anger with the horse-man took on such proportions that I feared the worst, should he ever make an appearance.

We entered Libohovë, passing between failed attempts at high-rise flats. We stopped on an unpaved square, in the shadow of thick plane trees, in front of a stylish old building that extended the full width of the square, and with a gateway in the middle. On the ground floor, I could see something that looked like a shop, with a space next door containing only a billiard table, and a little further along, a bar. Outside, on imitation Thonet chairs, sat the men of the village – the women remained invisible for the time being. One of the regulars looked at us provocatively through an open window. That didn't bode well. There were only boys playing in the square. When I took out my camera, they all wanted to be in the picture, hanging together with their arms around each others' shoulders, like a tired football team. As everyone continued to stare at me, I walked through the gateway and found myself in the inner courtyard of a dilapidated Albanian mansion. The Albanian flag hung limply above the front steps, which were covered in climbing plants.

Through the gateway, I could hear the sound of men's voices raised in agitation. I walked back to see Karagjozi, small but brave, facing up to a man of the same height, but with a broad, wild head that suggested that he was a descendant of hordes from the steppes, who had appeared on the scene at some time in the distant past and then disappeared again just as quickly, leaving behind clouds of dust and illegitimate children.

'The horse-man,' sighed Daniël.

Karagjozi was spitting fire, while the horse-man made defensive gestures. The other men on the square watched the argument closely, apparently finding it completely normal. I always get nervous if differences of opinion lead to a lot of shouting. The opponents continued, as though a mechanism had been set in motion that could no longer be stopped. I paced back and forth on the square. If it went on like this, we wouldn't have a horse-man at all. How would we carry on with the journey?

Suddenly, it fell quiet. They had separated while I wasn't looking. Karagjozi came over to me, his face grim. 'Impossible to talk to him,' he growled. 'Impossible. He's a madman, a complete idiot.'

'Why wasn't he there this morning?' I asked.

'He claims that the horses were too slow, but I said to him: you should have thought of that. If necessary you could have left in the middle of the night.'

'So what now?'

'I want nothing more to do with this man.' The professor waved a hand in the air, as if to remove the man from his sight. 'You can't agree anything with him.'

I remembered what Hobhouse wrote about problems with horses: 'These difficulties occurred every day of our travels, and we never were less than two hours getting fairly on our journey – a delay sufficient to try the patience of the most enduring temper.'

We sat down at a free table outside the bar. The mayor came to introduce himself. He was an amiable man with light-blue eyes, though this in itself was a guarantee of nothing, if Ali Pasha were anything to go by. The mayor seemed to have a reconciliatory effect; the tension eased and the beer did the rest. Only the professor continued to sit with his arms firmly crossed and an angry furrow across his brow. But he was forced to abandon his sombre thoughts when he was once again called upon to show his skills as in interpreter. Three teachers joined us. I noticed their refined features. They were marked by deprivation – perhaps more mental than material – and a shroud of endless sadness hung around them.

The mayor told us that the imposing building and the mansion in the courtyard used to belong to Mufit-Bey Libohovë, who was related to Ali Pasha. His descendants had been dispossessed by the Communists, after which they had gone into exile. One branch of the family lived in France, and another in America. Under new laws in the young democracy, they could reclaim their properties. None of the original exiles was still living, but one of the heirs had already come to take a look.

I excused myself and stood up, curious to see the shop. I wondered what would be on sale in a mountain village on the edge of Albania? There were no basic necessities, like fruit, vegetables or milk. The shelves offered a wide range of articles that put me in mind of a market or fair: clothing of the cheapest quality, lamps, vases, combs, sweets. And, for the first time since we arrived in the village, I saw a woman. She was standing behind the counter, smiling from ear to ear. I couldn't leave without buying something, so I pointed to a school exercise book and a roll of froufrou. Too late, I realised that I had no *leks*. I called the professor to lend me the money, but when he took out his wallet, her gestures made it clear that she didn't want me to pay anything. Embarrassed, I shook my head. 'I just want to pay for them,' I persisted. It was an awkward situation: two women who insisted on doing each other a favour. Karagjozi grasped my arm and said: 'You have to accept. She wants to give them to you.' I gave up, thanked her effusively, and left the shop with a terrible feeling of guilt.

The soft-cover exercise book came from France. It was a faded green *Tigre-Cahier* of low quality. On the back were the times tables from one to 12, Roman numerals and a *Division de Temps*. From a century, 100 years, to a minute, 60 seconds. Dividing up time seemed so easy. It only became difficult when you tried to bridge 200 years. When did they stop using these exercise books in France? In other words, when would they have been dumped in Albania?

The horse-man strolled over to us, looking a little timorous. We found a chair for him. Karagjozi stared pointedly at the ground.

'He's here now with the horses. Let's give him another chance,' I said softly. 'He messed up today, but he might do better tomorrow. Good horse-men don't grow on trees.'

He nodded slowly. He had come to the same conclusion. But it was the fact that he was dependent on this barbarian that upset him so much.

I had thought of a compromise, and now suggested it cautiously. How about if, the next morning, we drove back to Peshkepi by car. Then we could do the second part of the route to Libohovë, which we had not yet done because of lack of time, on foot. We could then leave Libohovë on horseback in the afternoon.

The horse-man watched us, wide-eyed. He knew that we were

talking about him. Daniël thought it was a good idea. Eventually, Karagjozi resigned himself to the idea. Peace was struck between him and the horse-man, but the furrow remained. Half-heartedly, they shook each others' hand.

The mayor felt that something official should now happen. He suggested a guided tour of the library, which was housed in the town hall. We took our leave of Ilyás and his colleague, who unloaded our rucksacks. In a small procession, we passed under the balcony with the flag into the building. I could see now that there were weeds growing between the roof tiles, and the plaster on the walls was peeling. We traipsed through the mouldered building in a line. The books were grimy and damp – before long they would start to decompose of their own accord. In one corner, there were piles of posters with martial-sounding slogans designed to raise the awareness of the workers. French classics stood fraternally next to the works of Lenin. One of the teachers took Professor Karagjozi's book about you off the shelf and opened it. At the front there was a quotation by Enver Hoxha. He went to tear it out, looking questioningly at the Professor. The latter nodded. 'You didn't have any choice, then,' he said laconically.

We entered the council chamber and automatically followed the example of the mayor, who took a seat at the long meeting table. Our company had in the meantime grown. All kinds of people joined us at the table and sat in anticipation, with solemn expressions on their faces. They had one thing in common: they were all members of the male sex. Apart from the shop assistant, I hadn't seen a single woman. Where were the women of Libohovë?

We all sat there in silence. Apparently nothing had been prepared for this official gathering. All eyes were directed towards us, full of expectation, three travellers from far away who were following your tracks, which happened to pass through their village. To put a stop to the collective silence, I started asking random questions: 'Have any of you read anything by Byron? Do you know why he travelled through Albania?'

A small man with dark skin and frizzy hair spoke up: 'I have been crazy about Lord Byron since secondary school,' he said, with a shy laugh. 'That he praised Albania fills me with pride. I am very fond of his style and…', he faltered for a moment, 'his melancholy, because I am like that, too.' A passionate admirer, here on the margins of Europe! 'Then you should have joined the Byron Society long ago,' I said. Karagjozi nodded hesitantly. We both knew that the Society in Albania was on its last legs and that he single-handedly kept it alive.

'This gentleman is hereby appointed an honorary member of the Byron Society,' said Karagjozi magnanimously.

The man beamed. Hilarity spread around the table and everyone became very animated. Only the teachers continued to radiate gloom. One of them told me that the Mufit-Bey family had possessed a richly stocked library, which most probably included antiquarian copies of your work. But, he ended sadly, the Communists had burned all the books.

His colleague said that we should see the ruins of the castle, higher up the mountain above Libohovë. He told us that, at the time of your journey, it was inhabited by one of Ali Pasha's sisters. On the day that you and Hobhouse arrived in Libohovë, her son was getting married and there was a great feast. The entire village still knew that you had been there and had stayed the night. Is that true? Were you at the wedding? I doubt it, otherwise one of you would have mentioned it. It seems more likely to me to be an apocryphal tale, or just wishful thinking. True or not, we all left the chamber and headed up the mountain.

Only the battlements were still there, but the mansion that had stood within the walls, where grandfather Mufit-Bey had lived, had been demolished. By the Communists again. We climbed the battlements. The sky became redder. While everyone admired the view over the valley and an elongated lake far below us, Daniël – a born sceptic – growled: 'Everything used to be the fault of the Turks. Now, it's the Communists.'

*Dichtung und Wahrheit*, fiction and truth, started to become all mixed up together. To me, the best part of the ruin was a black pig rooting around in the ground and a prehistoric tractor that looked like a creation by Tinguely, hanging together by improvisation, half a century of political aid brought together in the form of Russian and Chinese components. It started to get dark quickly. I didn't notice that the rest of the group had already sounded the retreat, and was still standing looking at the pig when I heard the sound of car doors closing. The animal looked at me with its small, sly eyes. I took off my fez and bowed: 'Ali is great...'

In a chauffeur-driven car, which the mayor used everyday to go back and forth to work, we drove higher and higher along a terrifyingly narrow road without a crash barrier and a bottomless drop on one side. Afrim Karagjozi announced that we were to spend the night at the mayor's house. We came to another part of Libohovë where what looked like the better houses stood behind high walls. The mayor had a new house built in traditional style. In the living room, there were Turkish-style divan sofas against three of the walls. The fourth wall was covered by a large wall unit, containing a television, that was to stay on all evening, and a portable cassette recorder, flanked by upright cassettes, by way of decoration. Everywhere, there were vases of artificial flowers, while the divan covers also displayed patterns of hand-sized flowers.

We were introduced to the mayor's family: his wife, four children, a grandchild and a grandmother of 86. The women disappeared immediately back into the kitchen, except for grandma, who had long ago become exempt from the separation of the sexes and sat unmoving and half blind in a corner of the room. The raki was already on the table. I, as the only woman, was served a glass of sickly sweet pink liqueur. A son-in-law and a neighbour joined us at the table. The mayor's wife came shyly into the room with salad, aubergines and rice biscuits, and disappeared again.

While we were eating, I wondered how I might be able to talk to the grandmother. Born three years before the end of the Turkish occupation, she bore the weight of the whole of 20th-century Albanian history on her shoulders. I turned to Afrim Karagjozi: 'Can I ask the old lady something?' He glanced absent-mindedly in grandma's direction, as though he had only just realised that she was there. 'Of course.'

'How does she feel about living in her son's house?'

Karagjozi translated the question.

Grandmother, from her vantage point on a sofa in her corner, nodded. 'I have only started to live in the past five years, since this house was built. Before that, it was nothing but misery.'

Her son took over the story. First, half her family had been killed in the war. Later, when Enver Hoxha was in power, her husband and her brother were considered anti-Communist elements, because they were patriots. Their house was destroyed because it was too bourgeois and the whole family was interned in a primitive camp near Tepelene. In 1955, her husband and eldest son managed to escape to America, leaving her behind with four daughters and a son. It was agreed that, as soon as the circumstances made it possible, she would follow her husband across the ocean. But he died before it could happen. Only the son had survived in the New World. She had recently seen him in Greece again for the first time in 40 years. Later, the family was given permission to return to Libohovë. At first they lived in the house of a Communist uncle and, as punishment for the milieu to which they had once belonged, were forced to work on the digging of the lake – the same lake over which the sun had set so beautifully that evening. That meant that, every day, they had to go down the mountain and climb back up again at the end of the day – a walk of two hours down and at least two back up. It was only since Albania had become a democracy and her son had been able to build this house that life had acquired a little colour.

Grandmother listened closely. Now and again, she would nod in agreement: it had happened just as her son had told it.

The meal we were then served took up all our attention. On a round baking tray more than half a metre across was a pie of puff pastry, lamb and rice. How large must their oven be? We showered our hostess with compliments: where had she learned to prepare such an impressive dish? She blushed and her husband replied: 'My mother taught her to cook. She made her learn all her recipes and if it was not good, she would give her a good roasting.' Everyone laughed, including the weary-looking cook. A bottle of Albanian wine was uncorked, a 1986 Kallmet. As Daniël and I thirstily emptied our glasses, I noticed that no one else was drinking. Was wine a luxury? I started to wonder if we had not unwittingly demanded too much of the household budget. Should we pay for this, or did it fall under the traditional law of hospitality? It was something I had not yet discussed with Karagjozi.

'Nothing remains of the wine industry in Albania,' said the professor, sombrely staring at the label. This complaint gave rise to a series of jokes about the former regime, which was blamed for everything. They particularly had it in for Dulla the Ugly and Sorra the Crow, favourite nicknames for Enver Hoxha and his consort.

After the meal, the women gradually came into the room. Without a sound, they joined grandma in the corner. One of the daughters, who I guessed was about 16, wore a T-shirt with the provocative text: Wounded but dangerous Lion. 'Do you know what that means?' I asked her.

She shyly shook her head. Karagjozi translated it for her, sniggering a little. A young Albanian with such a text on her chest confused him. He told me later, that he had forbidden his wife to wear jeans.

Forbidden was perhaps a little strong, he added. 'I told her I didn't like it, so she didn't do it.' The girl laughed, satisfied; she liked the meaning of the text. Perhaps it referred to a strength that has lain dormant for centuries in these women, who always remain in the background. One day, Frossini would be avenged.

Through the excess of drink and food, I felt pleasantly intoxicated. I remained at the table as long as I felt it necessary out of politeness, but then thanked our hosts for the delicious meal and retired to the bedroom that had been allocated for Daniël and myself. Karagjozi, embroiled in a heated political discussion, held his ground, pale with exhaustion.

I rinsed away the dust of the journey in a dingy, white-tiled bathroom that was already, only five years after the house had been built, starting to show signs of wear. The bath had dents in it, and the sealant had been carelessly applied everywhere. I did not know then that having a bathroom was in itself a rare luxury that the family would be proud of. With a sigh of contentment, I slid between the sheets. At last, a bed. But what a bed! Just as I was ready to snuggle up comfortably, I realised that the mattress would never allow that to happen, no matter which way I turned. It was lumpy, damp and most probably home to a wide variety of hidden insect life. It was filled, I knew without closer inspection, with a coagulation of ancient kapok, saturated with bodily fluids and house mites. The mattress had a long history of births, conceptions, menstrual cycles, bed-wetting, incontinence and terminal breaths. Now I could not sleep; I could imagine all these primal expressions of human existence in their full glory in my mind's eye. Meanwhile, the sheets, no matter how deeply I tucked them in on the left side of the bed, continually slid off on the right. And there was a penetrating marshy smell in the room that permeated to the depths of my lungs every time I breathed in.

Some people are robbed of their clothes and left naked and alone in the mountains, I told myself.

I thought of us trudging through Hoxha's defence bunkers, wading through the river, and peeling pomegranates. Was Albania different? Yes. In my stomach, my first Albanian meal was starting to make itself felt, accompanied by burping and indigestion. Had I eaten too heartily? Every time a new dish had been placed in front of me, I had filled my plate again with an almost suicidal politeness. I do not eat much, and I sleep a lot. That was now being forcibly reversed.

Daniël came to bed and immediately fell into a blissful sleep. He was the real traveller of the two of us, you could hear that by his deep and regular breathing. Could I not sleep because I was nervous, or was I nervous because I could not sleep? Sort that one out, so far from home. Tomorrow you have to be well rested, I told myself. Come on, sleep! But it was as though someone held a pistol against my chest and ordered me to relax.

Perhaps it would help if I were to empty my bladder. Without putting on a light, I crept into the hall. The door to the living room was wide open. To my great consternation I saw the whole family, driven from their beds by their guests, rolled up in blankets asleep. On the sofas against the walls, on the floor in the middle of the room. Everyone had sacrificed their own comforts to make us comfortable, and I was stalking though the house like Edward Rochester's mad wife in *Jane Eyre*. I was ashamed. Why did I have such little faith in the order of things?

Eventually, I sought refuge in a solution that did not exist in your time: a capsule containing liquid gold. If you swallow it, you are lulled into an artificial sleep from which you awake five hours later, perhaps not refreshed but less out of sorts than if you had not slept at all.

But I was not be granted my full five hours. My alarm clock went off an hour too early – I had forgotten to change it to Albanian time. The whole house was still intensely quiet. How those Albanians could sleep! Again, I was the only one creeping around the house. It was still half-dark in the bathroom, but pressing the light switch did not mean that the light came on. Did they have no electricity at night? To let in a little of the early morning light, I carefully opened the window... At that precise moment, three dogs threw themselves at my throat, as if they had spent hours waiting with glee to scare the living daylights out of an innocent stranger in the morning twilight. I jumped backwards. Cupping my trembling hands, I splashed a little water onto my face, but it didn't help against the sleeping pill that was still keeping me in a state of stupefaction. As I got dressed, I felt a slight cramp in my stomach. 'Everything's fine,' I told my reflection in the mirror.

From a number of Hobhouse's comments, I gather that your night in Libohovë was also not without its discomforts: 'At the house of this Turk [a relation of one of Ali's wives], in an outer room, separated from the chambers which contained his family, we were lodged during our stay in Libokavo, and the good-humoured Mussulman endeavoured to render us as comfortable as possible. [...] but we were not well-lodged during the night, for the whole party, thirteen in number, slept in the same room with us, as, this being a Turkish town, we could not procure quarters for our attendants in any other house.'

Although you were no stranger to hypochondria, you did not complain at all during this journey. Did the experience elevate you above yourself? Had you already crept into the role of *Childe Harold*? A paper hero feels nothing. In any case, in your letters and journals you do present a very tough and invulnerable image of yourself. During a storm one night aboard ship, while the sails were ripped to shreds and the captain burst into tears, you wrapped yourself in your Albanian cloak and 'lay down on deck to await the worst. I have learnt to philosophise in my travels...'

If only I did not start resembling your servant Fletcher: 'He has suffered nothing but from cold, heat, and vermin, which those who lie in cottages and cross mountains in a cold country must undergo, and of which I have equally partaken with himself; but he is not valiant.'

Valiant, yes, that's what I wanted to be.

# Chapter 9

WHY DID I FEEL such a need to travel? Why was it for Byron almost a matter of life and death that he left England? In *Travellers to an Antique Land*, Robert Eisner wonders what it is that makes people 'set out on the road [...] and abandon the comforts of a residence and a routine. Are the local cooking and the nervous tension worth it?'

Eisner offers the opinions of a number of renowned and experienced travellers. Bruce Chatwin, who was fascinated by the last nomads and shared their lives for a time, was convinced that human restlessness was 'a migratory drive, inseparable from our central nervous system'. The so-called blessings of a settled existence bring a whole string of responsibilities that nomads are spared. The words of Robert Louis Stevenson, written a century earlier in *Travels with a Donkey*, seem to confirm Chatwin's suspicions: 'For my part, I travel not to go anywhere, but to go. I travel for travel's sake.' More in Byron's style, Robert Burton wrote in *The Anatomy of Melancholy*: 'No better physic for a melancholy man than change of air and variety of places, to travel abroad and see fashions.' In *Travel – And Escape from Your Friends*, Evelyn Waugh believes that irritable writers need to get away from time to time or 'go off their heads'. Because they do not have a job away from home, they live in an invariable, almost symbiotic relationship with friends, family and the daily routine. The dangers of habit are aptly expressed by the Russian formalist Viktor Shklovsky. Habit, he says, 'devours objects, clothes, furniture, one's wife and the fear of war.'

The controversial French writer Gabriel Matzneff who, as a genuine admirer of the person and the poet (in that order), studied a number of Byron's 'idiosyncrasies' – including his tendency to fast on a regular basis – presented a rather eccentric theory in his book

*La diététique de Lord Byron*: travel as an alternative to suicide. 'Voluntary death frees us; travel does the same. Throwing oneself from the cliffs at Dieppe or taking the plane to Manila – they are more or less the same.' Matzneff suggests that, together with poetry and love, travelling prevented Byron from committing suicide. From an early age, Byron was prone to attacks of deep melancholy that might have driven others to suicide. In May 1811, on the way back to England, he wrote: 'At twenty-three, the best of life is over and its bitters double.' At that age, you could suspect him of flirting with the romance of *Weltschmerz*, but ten years later he suffered feelings of depression almost daily: 'I have been considering what can be the reason why I always wake, at a certain hour in the morning, and always in very bad spirits – I may say, in actual despair and despondency, in all respects – even of that which pleased me over night.'

Furthermore, Matzneff shares the widely held opinion that Byron's travelling was both an escape and the realisation of a boyhood dream. It was an escape from his Puritan country of birth, where he was not free to express his natural tendencies (homosexual relations still carried the death penalty), from his creditors, from the disillusionments of love, from the hostility and scorn of the critics. 'Putting a distance between you and the women who have betrayed you,' says Matzneff, 'between yourself and those who write unpleasant things about you, between yourself and the worries of the world, is to create a virgin, non-consummated state; to be less vulnerable.' After a malicious piece had been written about his *Hours of Idleness* in the Edinburgh Review, Byron wrote to Henry Drury: 'The Mediterranean and the Atlantic roll between me and criticism; and the thunders of the Hyperborean Review are deafened by the roar of the Hellespont.' In Persia, he promised, he would light his pipe with the article. The perspective of distance. Eleven years later, when living in Ravenna, he asked his publisher John Murray not to send him any more newspaper articles or any comments at all on his work – he preferred to stay out of reach of the tentacles of literary England.

Matzneff sees him as eternally searching for a safe place, where 'sorrow cannot reach', a paradise where life is carefree and sensual, and love is free. Where else could that be than in the Mediterranean Orient, amidst the Greeks, Romans and Turks he had dreamed about as a boy? On the coasts of the *Mare Nostrum*, where his warm-blooded, passionate nature was more at ease than in the cold, sober *Inglaterra*? His longing for the South and his alienation from his mother country had already started when he still wore short trousers and breathlessly read the history of the Romans and the Turks. There was good reason why he dressed himself as a Turkish boy whenever he had the chance. The desire to leave was there long before his actual departure. In the words of Robert Eisner: '... for if one feels a stranger at home, then abroad, where strangeness is automatically legitimised, is a far more comfortable place to vacation, even to live and work.' Byron's Grand Tour only served to increase his alienation: when he returned to England, he actually wanted to leave again immediately.

And why do I myself feel the need to travel regularly? To escape from myself, I think, and the daily environment that is part of my history. I travel into the unknown, freed from the past and the future, to become someone else who is open to whatever I encounter: I become a sponge, absorbing impressions. Under the influence of the situations that occur and the people I meet, I change, even though now and again – especially when the going is tough – I am mercilessly confronted by the old me, which I thought I had left safely at home.

My journeys are also an escape from the pressure cooker of the modern age. I can no longer keep up, bear the tension. The present is too noisy. Where is the silence? Has another Prometheus stolen it? Feverishly, I seek a way back into the past – looking for a house that looks like the houses children draw, with a plume of smoke from the chimney and a tree in the garden. I am too old, or too old-fashioned, for the modern world.

In the deepest sense, I travel to lose control over my life and to come closer to that one truth: that life is dangerous and changeable and that I do not know my fate. Strangely enough, I can then breathe more freely.


ALTHOUGH THE TONE of Byron's letters during his first journey is exceptionally light-hearted, sometimes even euphoric ('I am vastly happy and childish'), his reflections on the way 'home' testify to an advanced degree of morbidity:

> '[Four or Five Reasons in Favour of a Change]
> B. Malta 22 May 1811
> 1stly, at twenty three the best of life is over and its bitters double.
> 2ndly I have seen mankind in various Countries and find them

equally despicable, if anything the Balance is rather in favour of the Turks.

3rdly I am sick at heart:

"Me jam nec *faeminam*
Nec *Spes animi credula mutui*
Nec *certare* juvat *Mero*."*

[*Note: Byron does not quote Horace (to Venus) entirely correctly here from memory:

"Nor maid nor youth delights me now,
Nor credulous dream of heart's exchange, nor hours
of challenged wine-bout, nor the brow
Girt with a wreath of freshly gathered flowers"]

4thly A man who is lame of one leg is in a state of bodily inferiority which increases with years and must render his old age more peevish & intolerable. Besides in another existence I expect to have two if not four legs by way of compensation.

5thly I grow selfish and misanthropical, something like the jolly miller – I care for nobody – no not I – and nobody cares for me.

6thly My affairs at home and abroad are gloomy enough.

7thly I have outlived all my appetites and vanities – aye even the vanity of authorship.'

To Henry Drury he wrote: 'I mean to give up all connection, on my return, with many of my best friends – as I supposed them – and to snarl all my life. But I hope to have one good-humoured laugh with you, and to embrace Dwyer, and pledge Hodgson, before I commence cynicism.'

Here the facetious, sometimes grim and melancholic mood of many of his later letters is already in evidence. It is this tone, revealing a self-knowledge that sometimes degenerates into self-mockery, that I find so captivating and which shows that, in his letters and perhaps also in his daily life, he was hardly the romantic that people wish to see in him, but a realist with a keen insight into himself and the human race as a whole.

# Chapter 10

M Y DEAR FRIEND, Daniël, the true traveller of the two of us, got up rested. He had had no problems at all. Our hostess brought us bread, goats' cheese and mountain tea – I drank only the tea, to try and calm the rumbling in my stomach.

And then began the wait for the Mercedes that would take us back to Peshkepi. We wandered around the house. As far as I could see, there were shady gardens with fruit trees and top-heavy haystacks. Shouting loudly in Illyrian, the mayor's wife drove two sleepy cows into a meadow. We herded the whole family outside for a group photo – only the aged grandmother who had just started to enjoy her life did not manage to come out and pose for us so early.

Laborious puffing and rattling heralded the arrival of the Mercedes, as it toiled its way up the hill. We said our farewells, and made our promises. Attempts to express my gratitude for all the trouble they had taken to give us such a warm welcome evaporated, reduced to an incomprehensible stammer that Karagjozi had great difficulty in translating. As we went down the hill, I could see the lake again, far below us. We passed groups of schoolchildren with bags on their backs. We dropped the mayor off in the centre of Libohovë and Ilyás, who had received official permission to be our guide again that morning, took his place in the car.

In Peshkepi we continued the journey of the previous day. The path still ran along the flank of the mountains. To the left was the valley of the Drino with, on the other side, grey mountains with sharply defined curves, through which patches of sunlight shone. Very occasionally, we would encounter other people. Some had heavily laden donkeys, other were themselves bent double under large bundles of wood. When we explained our presence in this remote place, they nodded showing no signs of surprise. The women never went outside without their head scarves: was that a remnant of Islam, or for practical reasons? They inspected me, full of compassion, or pinched my arm encouragingly. Why is she not at home with her husband and children? I saw them thinking.

My stomach made its presence felt again. Obstinately, I focused my attention on the outside world – which changed in appearance with every step, up, down. In a village I saw a chestnut tree that must have been 100s of years old. Who had it seen come and go? Ali Pasha, King Zog, the Italians, the Germans, Enver Hoxha. Soldiers and merchants, villagers carried off into slavery, harem women in sedan chairs, robbers in sheepskins, curious travellers like you and Hobhouse – and us. It was tempting to attribute the tree wisdom and maturity and other human qualities.

'Many villages appear on the sloping sides of the surrounding hills,' said Hobhouse. That was still the case. Except that the use of the word 'hills' is in this case an enormous understatement. I admit that, in Holland, we do tend to call any slight elevation in the landscape a mountain, but the slopes that we climbed and descended were part of a large 'mound' 1,762 metres high.

In the villages, our path wound between walled gardens. Although the gardens within the walls were mostly clean and tidy, on the path we had to pick our way carefully between muddy puddles, rocks, horse and donkey droppings, and bags of rubbish that had been thrown over the walls. Poverty? No matter how poor you are, you can still collect the bags together and burn them outside the village, I thought, as a disinterested passer-by. In my country we had long ago devised collective solutions to problems like that, which everyone agreed to. But in post-Communist Albania, I had gathered from our dinner conversation the night before, there was a recalcitrant atmosphere of resistance against 50 years of collective solutions that almost no one had wanted.

'We were joined by a small party of Turks on horseback, one of whom pointed out, at a little distance from the snuff manufactory, a hill to the right, on which were, he said, the vestiges of ancient walls, as also some few other remains a little farther to the left, in a grove of trees. These I visited, and from the size of the stones, I should judge them to be antique: they were lying in heaps on the ground.'

'The vestiges of ancient walls', to the left of the road, were still there. Daniël examined them with an expert eye and concluded that they were the remnants of an Illyrian-Hellenic settlement. According to the Albanians, who claim to descend from them, the Illyrians were the first people to inhabit these parts, even before the Greeks and the Romans. They had come from the East and brought their own language with them. You and Hobhouse in effect travelled through here with a kind of tunnel vision – you only had eyes for Greek or Roman ruins and tried, like a pair of literary detectives, to identify cities, rivers, mountains and battlefields from mythology. An older civilisation, like the Illyrians, or a younger one, like that of Byzantium, fell outside your field of view.

That is why neither of you made any mention of the mosque next to the 'vestiges of ancient walls ... in a grove of trees'. It stood – and still stands – on a hill at the end of a drive lined with ancient cypresses. The trees cast dark shadows across the path, like sentinels with the patience of centuries. You could have jumped from one shadow to another. I found the mosque at the end of the green colonnade very appealing. Bunches of campanula hung from the cracks in the walls. In the overgrown garden, directly opposite the entrance, was a dome-shaped tomb. An old man came trudging up, delighted at this unexpected visit by fellow humans. In the tomb, he told us, lay the remains of a Bektashi priest who had lived and worked here his entire life. The man was now the last surviving retainer, engaged in a perpetual fight to preserve what was left against decay. We peered into the tomb. The coffin stood in the middle of the floor; on the Day of Judgment, the dead priest could simply step out of it again.

The man showed us round the mosque. There were only fragments left of the original frescos. It was unclear if they had been destroyed on Hoxha's orders, as Karagjozi blindly believed, or by time. Some arabesques were visible in the semi-darkness, only to disappear where they had originally continued in a mist of chalk. Here, the past had not been restored to oblivion, it was still there in the immeasurable silence between the high walls and pillars – untouched by the 20th century. There was an atmosphere of complete desolation, except perhaps for the restless souls of a few dervishes who were unable to take their leave of the place. We automatically spoke in reverent whispers. Dressed sheepskins hung drying sacrilegiously between the frescos. On the floor, instead of believers with their heads pointing towards Mecca, lay figs and silverskin onions.

On the first floor, out of respect, the priest's salon remained untouched. It was a harmonious room with a carved wooden ceiling and, on three sides, arched windows with white curtains, on which

Arabic characters had been embroidered. It was an Oriental room with multicoloured carpets on the floor and mattresses against the wall to sit or lie on. The sun filtered through the windows, as if trying to bring to life the scenes that had once taken place in there.

'This is where he would receive visitors,' said Karagjozi, his voice betraying both respect and rancour. Before we left I took a picture of him and Ilyás on the sickle-shaped steps at the entrance. The Professor made an attempt to smile, but the worried expression on his face looked as though it were there for good. Ilyás, who was wearing a brightly-coloured shirt especially for the occasion, had a slightly ironic smile, not surprising for a policeman who finds himself unexpectedly following in the tracks of someone who has been dead for 200 years, in the company of a pair of down-at-heel literary pilgrims.

As I pressed the shutter, I wished I was sitting on the steps myself. My stomach was rumbling so badly, that all I wanted to do was spend the rest of the day sitting with my head between my knees. I had resolved not to talk about it in this account, but now we are on the subject, I can only justify myself by appealing to your habit of filling pages in your letters and journals with the most gruesome details of your attacks of indigestion. You even devoted space to this obsession in your literary work. In *Don Juan* you refer to 'those who know what indigestion is – that inward fate which makes all Styx through one small liver flow'.

I managed to grin and stay upright, but thought it best to inform my travelling companions that the previous evening's meal had not agreed with me.

We carried on, passing meadows with haystacks in which gnomes lived, and fields of tobacco plants. Ilyás waited patiently for me every time the others disappeared behind the next bend in the mountain path until Karagjozi, who was starting to worry about my increasingly slow pace, felt the need to urge me on with a few comforting words: 'The people here think you are a brave woman, so be brave.' If you only knew how brave I am being, I thought, gnashing my teeth. I knew men who, in my condition, would lie down bent double under a plane tree, moaning, 'I'm dying, I'm dying!'.

At one point, at a sharp bend in the path, we nearly collided with an old woman in a flocked black woollen cardigan. Thin as a rake, she was knitting as she walked, taking no account of bumps or potholes in the path. It was as though her knit-one-purl-one made her somehow invulnerable. As she greeted us with a friendly nod, the clicking of the needles continued without hesitation. Perhaps she had a deal with the devil – as long as she continued knitting he would not come and claim her soul.

Just below the edge of a gorge, in an impossible spot, a bunch of yellow meadow saffron shone in the sun. I asked Karagjozi what they were called in Albanian. He didn't know, but before I could stop him he had squatted down dangerously on his haunches on the edge of the precipice, and reached down to pick the flowers. He had clearly forgotten that he had spent most of his life sitting at a table studying. 'I only wanted to know what they are called,' I said in a weak voice, but he didn't hear me.

He bent further and further, trying to reach that one last impossible flower.... Then he suddenly stood up, with a laugh full of bravura. Lightly dismissing my objections he pressed a bouquet into my hands.

'A flower for a flower,' he said gallantly.

And so we came to Libohovë, me with my posy and the Professor walking tall with pride. Suddenly, with youthful exuberance, he jumped over a fence. In a neglected garden, his hawk-eye had spotted wild cyclamen. He was now scared of nothing – in no time, he had gathered together a second bouquet. I tried to mutter something about leaving the flowers to grow where they were, but the words died on my lips. The cyclamen smelled of spring. With my double bouquet, I walked into the square where, the day before, peace had been struck between the Professor and the horse-man. We went into a post-Communist-style building, which we would today refer to as 'multifunctional'.

It was a restaurant, clubhouse and boarding house combined. It had a toilet you had to squat over and a washtub filled with ice-cold water. They served us meat with *pilaf*. I stuck to mountain tea. Because the waitress was so stern and dismissive, I suggested to Karagjozi that we give her the flowers – what use would I have for them on horseback? She accepted them with resignation. Obviously no one ever gave her flowers and she did not know how to respond. She also didn't know what the flowers were called. We consulted other people in the restaurant, but no one seemed to know the names of the plants that grew in and around the village. What they did know, better than me, were the names of Dutch footballers.

The Mercedes, which had arrived to bring our baggage and pick up Ilyás, carried us for the last time to the northern end of the village where – to our great amazement – the horse-man was waiting for us with three horses. The fourth horse, he mumbled, was inferior, and he had taken it back. One of the horses, a blond mare, looked at me questioningly. I succumbed immediately to the charms of this sister of Bucephalus. She would help me to conquer the mountains. One horse was reserved for the rucksacks. The third, a russet stallion which looked to have a more fiery temperament than the other two, would be ridden in turn by Karagjozi and Daniël. They were content with this compromise; I think that secretly neither was looking forward to spending the whole journey on horseback.

Our guide, whose name we never learned so that he would be known to us forever as 'the horse-man', was inexpertly trying to fix the rucksacks to the pack-saddle with straps. After Daniël had watched him for some time he cautiously suggested ways of distributing the weight better and tightening the straps so that they did not cut into the horse's side and that the load could not slide around. While he was living on Samos, Daniël had a donkey that he used as a pack animal. But the horse-man ignored his advice. His jaws, clenched shut, made it clear that he did not need any instructions from a foreigner. Daniël laughed, dumbfounded. Was this really a horse-man? The mayor of Libohovë had suggested him, and we knew nothing of his past record. 'I think he is a Vlach,' Daniël growled. I didn't know what that was, but it sounded like a curse.

Our attention was diverted to the Mercedes, where Professor Karagjozi was standing on the bonnet and trying to mount the russet stallion. It was unorthodox – his forefathers, the Shqiptars, had jumped straight into their saddles from the ground – but the result was the same. The Professor was in the saddle, but he didn't look too happy about it. It was a droll sight to see the little scholar sitting astride a warlike steed, a frown of mistrust on his face. Using a rock as a step-up, I sank into the saddle with a sigh of relief – I wouldn't have to walk another step. Ilyás waved us off with a concerned look on his face.

'On leaving Libokavo (October 17) we descended into the plain, and, before we could again get into our northern direction, were obliged to cross several wide and deep trenches, cut to drain the low grounds. After having regained our path for an hour and a half we came suddenly upon a rapid river flowing out of a valley in the mountains to the east in a westerly course, but soon turning to the north. As we were to pass the night in a village in the mountains to the right of our road, we were obliged to cross this river, which we accomplished with considerable difficulty [...]. After the passage of the stream we went over some deep ploughed lands, and, in three hours from Libokavo, began to ascend the hills in a north-westerly direction.'

We had to find our way with this description, conspicuous in its vagueness and contradictions. Where were we to begin with 'a rapid river flowing out of a valley in the mountains to the east in a westerly course, but soon turning to the north'? The horse-man knows the route, Karagjozi had been assured. At first, we walked through a valley, which seemed to fit the description. But soon the terrain started to get hilly, which confused us. Where was the rapid river that continually changed direction? At the foot of a mountain, on top of which the vague outlines of a ruin were visible – according to the map, the not yet excavated city of Antigoneia – the path seemed to fork off in two directions.

The Professor was certain that we should go to the left, while the horse-man was equally persistent that we were to go right. Both defended their own standpoints with great fervour. In the heat of this argument, Karagjozi slid off his horse. With both feet back on *terra firma*, he could concentrate better. What followed, as far as we could make out, was an exchange of Albanian expletives.

'What is he saying?' I shouted to Karagjozi every now and again.

But he signalled to me to be silent with a firm: 'Let me handle this.'

I dismounted and went to sit in the grass, resigned to wait. From nowhere, a young policeman suddenly appeared. Had he come from the nearest village because they were dubious about our venture? He, too, quickly realised that it would be best to sit and wait. Karagjozi was waving his baseball cap, which had given him such a martial appearance on his horse, resolutely to the west, while the horse-man waved to the east with the umbrella he had brought along because the sky was so grey.

I took a picture at the moment when the disagreement erupted. You can see Daniël between the two warring parties, with an incredulous smile on his face, unaware that it would soon be wiped off.

It began to dawn on us that, when Albanian men disagree, they shout at each other. They do their best to make their voices sound masculine, stare at each other in outrage and contempt, unable to comprehend the stupidity of the other, walk away angrily, and then come back. It is an age-old tradition of mutual intimidation that, not so long ago, was settled with a dagger, or by the surrender of one of the parties.

Now it was the Professor's turn to walk away – but this time he did not come back. 'Follow me...!' he ordered us, calling over his shoulder. But we unfolded the map and tried again to retrace your route. To us, it seemed that the horse-man was right, and that we should turn right into the mountains and then northwards towards Qesarat, the village where we planned to spend the night.

The figure of the Professor seemed to get smaller and smaller. He was striding resolutely along the path, followed a little uncertainly by the policeman. 'Follow me...', we heard him call once more, but let him go – he was in good company. We would have liked to climb up to Antigoneia, but there was no time. It was too uncertain how long we would take to cover the distance. We climbed back onto our horses and entered a broad path that ran alongside a stream a little further along. Was this the river Hobhouse mentioned? Here, too, there had been a forest fire. 'The herders light the fires,' said Daniël. 'They think it is good for the soil.'

Riding a horse is definitely superior to walking. The walker, in hiking boots that bear the names of famous peaks, is forced to continually keep one eye on the path. A loose rock, a badly judged leap, a slippery slope – the view is much less spectacular from the bottom of a gorge.... And the second day, your calf muscles ache from all the climbing, and your stomach muscles from all the going down.

How different it is on horseback. All you have to do is sit. It is exactly the right height to survey the surrounding panorama at your ease. You sway gently through the landscape, leaving the state of the path to the horse, which sets every hoof down with the greatest of care. Sitting on the warm back of a living beast, for a long time in human history the only way to move from place to place, felt very familiar to me. It would not surprise me if, somewhere in the depths of our cerebral cortex, there is still a rudiment of our long-gone ancestors, galloping over the steppes.

Had I perhaps benefited from my lessons in the English trot and canter, all those years ago in the pine forests of Brabant? Hardly, because here, the horse moved forward hoof by hoof. But once, in a meadow near a stream, my horse suddenly had an attack of high spirits and broke into an awkward trot. I was tossed from side to side in the wooden pack-saddle, designed to carry jute sacks and wicker baskets. This was no racehorse, she was used to the mountains. All I had to do was make sure I didn't fall off. But she was so good-natured! The soft blonde mane, the throbbing muscle in her neck, the docile way that she obeyed the slightest pull on the reins, the naturalness with which she watched over my safety. They say that the front end of a horse does not know the back end even exists. But that is a fable. My horse knew exactly where she and I started and ended.

Disturbingly, the path and the river suddenly curved to the right, while we should have gone to the left and upwards to stay in the right direction. The path petered out. We forced our way through thorny bushes and low, overhanging branches – I had to keep stopping to pick them out of my hair.

Concerned about the route we were following, Daniël suddenly took umbrage and disappeared from sight. Only the horse-man was now in front of me, on the horse with the baggage. On his back, the black umbrella hung like a bat on the collar of his jacket. Now and again he would rein in his horse to pass me a maggoty apple or a mouldy walnut. While he did this, he said things I didn't understand, accompanied by gestures that mean different things in different countries. He pressed a spot under one eye, and then the other, with his middle finger, all the time staring at me closely. Or he pointed with his hand to a spot halfway up his thigh. Did that mean, the others are mad, forget about them? Or was it an indecent proposal? Daniël's comment that he was probably a Vlach, now seemed to have some sinister meaning. What was that, a Vlach? His cheeks and chin were covered in stubble. I guessed he was about 50, but he could have been much older or younger – what effect did the fresh Albanian mountain air have on the appearance? He acted as though we shared a secret, which did not please me at all. Looking at him intently, I tapped my watch: enough nonsense, we have to make haste. 'The Professor...?' he asked. The Professor, I nodded.

Was he insulted? Without warning, he took off after Daniël, whose silhouette had appeared again in the distance. He suddenly seemed to be taking pleasure in shouting orders at Daniël in a gruff tone: left here, right there. Daniël became very nervous and his clothes got caught on twigs and thorns. What kind of idiot had we been entrusted to? A guide who was not a guide, a horse-man who was not a horse-man? He had no idea of the route we should be following, that much was clear. 'Don't shout at me!' Daniël yelled at him. He was becoming a real Albanian.

The slope became steeper and steeper; it felt as though the ground would disappear from beneath my feet at any moment. To our right, at the bottom of a gaping gorge, was the winding stream that was our only landmark. I started to doubt the infallibility of my honest mare. Now and again her hooves would slip, scraping on the rock, and I could feel every muscle in her body seeking to regain her balance. I was ready to jump. At the most dangerous spots she would stop and, with complete disregard for her safety, start munching at a tasty shrub. The horse-man had given me a twig to whip her with, but I would rather have used it as a toothpick.

While the horse was tearing off leaves with rapid, biting movements, I looked around. We had reached quite a height, and the view behind us had changed. Far below, with a single stroke of his light-blue brush, the Grand Master had added a lake, below that in green, the valley of the Drino, and in the background, in a hazy grey-blue, the mountains on the other side. He had moved the clouds to one side, so that the late-afternoon sun – setting too fast for comfort – could light up the folds in the mountains. The outline of Antigoneia was silhouetted sharply against the sky, to attract an audience for the heavenly chorus that would fill the air as darkness fell.

You wrote in a letter to your friend Henry Drury: 'Albania, indeed, I have seen more of than any Englishman [...], for it is a country rarely visited, from the savage character of the natives, though abounding in more natural beauties than the classical regions of Greece, – which, however, are still eminently beautiful, particularly Delphi and Cape Colonna in Attica. Yet these are nothing to parts of Illyria and Epirus, where places without a name, and rivers not laid down in maps, may, one day, when more known, be justly esteemed superior subjects, for the pencil and the pen, to the dry ditch of the Ilissus and the bogs of Boeotia.'

You were right, this landscape was a 'superior subject for the pen'. And yet its beauty was difficult to capture in words. So I took a photograph, an alternative that was not yet at your disposal if words were inadequate. Although I was hanging sideways and half back-to-front on my horse, this picture turned out to be one of the most beautiful photos I have ever taken. There is no indication at all that the photographer was lost and suffering from a dicky tummy, except perhaps indirectly in the great contrast – reminiscent of Rembrandt – between light and dark.

Unexpectedly, the horse-man once again raised his voice. He was calling the Professor – and received an answer. But where from?

Because of the echo caused by the mountainsides, it seemed to come from all directions. Had Karagjozi become, like God, omnipresent? The horse-man looked at me, his eyebrows raised, and pointed his umbrella towards Antigoneia. He seemed to think the Professor's voice came from there, so why not go and take a look? I shook my head, pointing to the sun. It would be ridiculous to go back, even higher, just to see if it really was the Professor who had called.

We laboured on until we came to what may have been a path. Was it the right path? We didn't know anymore, all we wanted to do was to get back before dark. The horse-man was still exceptionally inventive in creating confusion. Now he kept stopping to call the Professor. Perhaps he had started to have doubts about who his boss was, who was going to be paying him. The voice called back again, suddenly much closer. There was no doubt at all now, it was definitely the Professor. We crossed a field with small piles of stones, evenly spaced. Was this a mystical site, where Illyrian rites were conducted at full moon? On the other side Karagjozi stood waiting for us, staring grimly into the low sun.

'Thies ies the wurst day of my haul life,' he said, gripping his chest near his heart. He had not needed his heart tablets in 15 years, but now he had had to take one. 'Why did you follow him, not me?' He could hardly contain his anger.

Because we thought that we had to go around Antigoneia to the right, we said timidly.

'I had the right path,' said Karagjozi, 'and I have also been to Antigoneia. I have been waiting for you here for an age. This idiot knows nothing. He is fired. I never want to see his face again.'

Later, when we looked at the maps again, we realised that we had both lost the way. You stayed on the plain longer and went into the mountains later than we did, passing to the left of Antigoneia, the existence of which you suspected: 'It [the Drino] is mentioned in Dr. Pouqueville's account as being the ancient Celydnus, and it may possibly be a branch of that river. With that supposition, the traveller might be inclined to look for some vestiges of Hadrianopolis, Amantia, and Antigonia; towns which flourished under the Romans, and which were placed somewhere in the country watered by the Celydnus.'

Pondering our sins, we rode along a sunken path lined with knotty trees. This was your path, I could feel that immediately. Here we came together again, we approached Qesarat as one. Copper-coloured light covered the landscape. In front of us, at a crossroads just before the village, Professor Karagjozi struck up a conversation with a number of villagers and two police officers, who had been sent from headquarters to see if the strangers had survived their journey through no-man's-land. The two policemen looked so alike that I thought I was seeing double from exhaustion.

A handsome young man – one who you would certainly have taken on as a page – came up to us. His foot was broken and was in plaster, and on his T-shirt there was a large winged letter A. What did it stand for? Antigoneia? Albania?

'What do you think of my country?' he asked in surprisingly good English.

'Beautiful,' I replied, nonplussed. 'The landscape is very impressive.'

'It's not that beautiful,' he countered. 'We are terribly poor.'

'Your soil is fertile. You could develop farming, and tourism,' I suggested. I felt a little haughty, talking down to him from on horseback.

'No, no,' he dismissed everything. 'There is no hope of starting anything here, everything here is impossible.'

The Professor felt called upon to say a few fatherly words to the boy.

'Albania is a rich country,' he declared with a certain pride. 'Rich in opportunities, if the people know how to take advantage of them, develop their own initiative.' With a broad gesture he presented all the potential opportunities. His meaning was clear: it was all possible, but the people themselves had to want it. He took his baseball cap off to wipe the sweat from his brow. What a day it had been! One ordeal after the other. Now, on top of everything, he had to try and arouse the fighting spirit of the younger generation, too.

But the boy just kept shaking his head. He worked in Greece. Unfortunately he had broken his foot and couldn't work for a while, but after it had healed he would go back as soon as possible. Karagjozi accused him of escapism: there was work to be done here, building the country. What would happen to Albania if the young people left to go elsewhere? 'Please,' the young man interrupted him. 'I am talking to the lady.'

Turning his back on the Professor, he asked me if I could come back sometime. He wanted to show me an ancient church and a cave – this was an exceptional village. 'My name is Alexander,' he said proudly. 'Like Alexander the Great.' Aha, I thought, A for Alexander!

'Mirupafshim!' I heard people calling around us. Why were they saying goodbye? The whole time I had been labouring under the pleasant misapprehension that we had reached our destination, but this proved to be only Saraqinishtë. A terrible wave of exhaustion washed over me. Did we have to go even further? With vague promises, I said farewell to the winged A.

A few villagers who were more sturdy on their feet than he was accompanied us for a while, but turned back when a deep gorge gaped ahead of us, with exceptionally steep sides. Did we have to cross that? Yes, we did. You had done so. Everyone agreed, for a change, that this was exactly the course you and Hobhouse had followed. And yes, I remembered with trepidation, the following passage from Hobhouse's account: 'It had been very late before we recommenced our journey, so that after we had been in the hills an hour it grew dark. We mistook our path; the baggage-horses began to tumble; and, when we were half way up the mountain, we were obliged to stop in a wood, where we were bewildered and quite ignorant of our position. Two or three of us, however, determined to make for the first village and procure a guide, for we had been some time going up and down craggy precipices without seeming to advance towards our point.'

I held my breath and looked down. The gorge looked idyllic, full of smoke-trees with goat tracks winding between them. The red slopes were beautiful, but under these circumstances they gave the impression we would be descending into the fires of hell. It was so steep that we had to dismount and continue on foot, while the horseman took care of the horses.

I went down first, with only one thought in my mind: to get to the other side before dark. Now the sun had disappeared behind the mountains, everything started to quickly lose its colour. People, animals and objects would first turn grey, and then so black that you would no longer be able to distinguish them from each other. I would be feeling around in an impenetrable, smothering darkness.

So I rushed into the gorge ahead of the others, occasionally sliding down on rubble and loose rocks. Behind me I could hear the horses panting with the effort – 'the baggage-horses began to tumble'. If night overtakes us at the bottom of the gorge, I thought breathlessly, we won't be able to go a step further. You need light for every step on these small, rocky ledges. Then we will all be stuck together – an inflammable company full of smouldering recriminations that will spark into life in the darkness. I cannot even take out my contact lenses, because the holder and the liquid to keep them in are stored away in the deepest recesses of my rucksack, which is tied to the back of the horse with a thousand knots. That means I will have to keep my eyes open all night without seeing anything.

All these thoughts kept going through my head as I forced my way, sweating, through the smoke-tree forest. That you had got lost here too was no comfort. You could take the analogy too far. Since we were on the subject, another one came to me: 'Midway along the journey of our life, I woke to find myself in a dark wood, for I had wandered off from the straight path. How hard it is to tell what it was like, this wood of wilderness, savage and stubborn....' I was already past midway on the journey of my life. Perhaps the end was even near – I wouldn't be the first traveller to disappear without trace.

A steep wall of rock loomed in front of me. I had reached the other side of the valley, now I had to get up again. I could just make out a path – if it was a path at all – between the rocks. Pulling myself up in bushes and protruding rocks, I started to clamber upwards. My pulse was throbbing in my temples, my stomach pains returned with a vengeance. Mountains on a map are different to real mountains. Folded out on a table, they look deceptively innocent – fine curves in a darker shade of colour, their names printed next to them in letters, their heights in figures. In reality they are monstrous rocky bulges in the Earth's crust, many of them volcanic in origin. When they were created, little thought was given to making them accessible. A mountain is uncompromising. It refuses to budge. It doesn't care if you fall. You are mortal, the mountain is not. I became more aware of that arrogant indifference with every metre that I climbed.

By the time I reached the top, the gorge was in complete darkness. If I had taken five minutes longer, a long arm would have pulled me back down into Hades. Up here, too, night had fallen, but you could make out the silhouettes of houses and trees. Below me, I could hear from the sound of rolling rocks that the others were approaching. With my head full only of the dream image of a soft bed made up with smooth, clean sheets I stumbled on into the village without waiting for them. A dark being passed me silently with a flock of sheep. I pressed myself against the wall to allow the languidly swaying animals to pass – it was somehow calming.

I passed a house with a garden slightly higher than the road. A couple of children who were still playing outside saw me come shuffling past and let out shrill screams. Crying, they rushed into the house to fetch their father and older brother, who came running towards me across the garden, raging and cursing at me. Get away from here, how dare you come here and scare our children? At least, that was how I interpreted the noises they were making. I hurried away again, back the way I came. I was shocked, and indignant – I could never remember anyone being afraid of me before. I'm surprised that they didn't start throwing stones at me. I could still hear them swearing at me in the background, like thunder that is gradually moving away. But from the opposite direction, came the sound of voices.

Did I hear someone calling my name? Thank the gods, it was the others. They were angry, too. They had been calling my name for some time, to no avail. My legs were shaking, from fear, anger and fatigue. Like drowning persons, we entered the village together along another path. I told Karagjozi what had just happened to me. He didn't seem at all surprised.

'They think that you have the evil eye upon you,' he said laconically. 'Because you are a stranger, with blonde hair and light-coloured eyes, emerging suddenly from the darkness.'

The evil eye? An emissary from the devil? Would I perhaps have been lynched in former times? I burst out laughing – was I going mad?

'It's nothing to laugh about,' said the professor. 'I find it quite primitive.'

Our path came out near a building that, as far as we could see in the dark, was in an advanced state of decay. In front of it lay an old car on its side. In the light of the headlamps of another ancient car, lanky village youths were pushing the car back and forth until it was back on all four wheels, at which they all danced in triumph. There was no street lighting in any of the villages and the houses looked blacked-out as though in wartime, giving the scene a sinister appearance. As we watched from a distance, more and more curious men (always men) gathered around us, visible in the glowing ends of their cigarettes. Someone was sent to find our host and returned shortly afterwards with the news that he was ill and could not receive us.


OH NO! This was the last straw. My stomach responded immediately to this news. I sat down on a rock. 'Don't worry,' said the Professor. 'Let me handle this.' Above my head, negotiations took place in knotty language. It seemed to go on for hours. Everyone wanted to have their say, and no one was in a hurry. What were they cooking up? Were we going to have to sleep in the hay, here of all places, where I had already been branded an emissary of the devil? There was a jinx on this place. Across the valley I could see the lights of Gjirokastër beckoning. A clean hotel room, with a bed and a bath, all for me – seemingly close, but out of reach.

I tugged at Karagjozi's sleeve. 'Why don't we just take a taxi to Gjirokastër and sleep one night in a hotel, after the tough day we've had?'

But he dismissed the idea. 'No, no. I'll handle this, don't worry.'

I obviously needed a better argument, or we would still be standing here at midnight.

'Listen,' I insisted, standing up. 'I have to get to a dispensary. I need medicine for my stomach. The pain is starting to become unbearable.'

He hesitated. The villagers carried on talking. For them, we were the high point of the evening.

'OK, OK, we do that,' the Professor said suddenly. He even sounded relieved.

More negotiations. Someone had a car and was willing to take us, if we could agree on a price. It was by no means cheap, but we were in a compliant mood – we just wanted to get away from this ill-fated place. Again, two police officers appeared. How, I will never know. Without a car in any case, as they asked if they could drive with us to Gjirokastër.

Now all we had to do was rid ourselves of the horse-man. Karagjozi had seriously had enough of him and never wanted to see the man again – 'in my haul life'. We had not yet discussed a price. Because he had been recommended by the mayor, the Professor had simply assumed that the price would be reasonable.

From one moment to the next, the knotty language above my head turned into the roar of rusty cannons. The Professor and the horse-man were almost attacking each other physically, and everyone else was getting involved.

'What is the problem?' I shouted.

I should have known the answer. 'Let me handle this,' the Professor shouted back from the melee.

Groaning, I sank back down on to my rock.

I think that all the villagers had an opinion on the dispute. One after the other, they raised their voices, threateningly or indignantly. I don't know whose side they were on. They were a large clump of dark beings, swelling and contracting again, like a giant octopus.

'What's all the fuss about?' I kept shouting up at the Professor. Once, during a short lull in the proceedings, I received an answer.

'Money,' the professor called hoarsely. 'The man is asking a ridiculous price.'

'How much?' I persisted, but the shouting and shoving had resumed. Was this only my second evening in Albania? A sense of powerlessness, of the inability to act, gradually took hold of me. Was this perhaps how the Albanians felt in their lives, was it rubbing off on me? Or perhaps, how the women felt: waiting patiently while decisions were made for you?

'How much?' I kept calling weakly.

When they stopped to come up for air again, I heard: 'Four hundred dollars.'

My jaw dropped. For that amount, I knew, the Professor would have to teach for three months. I heard Daniël laugh ironically in the background. What on earth could the horse-man, with his stubble and his rotten apples, be thinking? That he had got himself the dream job of his life? Was he practising a modern version of highway robbery? Was he trying to make a rich Westerner feel guilty? Didn't he realise that a lot of people in the West would have to live for several weeks on that amount of money? Was it compensation for the fact that the Professor 'never wanted to see him again in his haul life'? Or was he just being naive, and thought it sounded like a nice round number? Was it overconfidence or stupidity? I suspected the latter. And in that case, there was no point in discussing it with him.

'Let's just go now and talk about it again in the morning,' I called, standing up again.

Karagjozi, who was probably on the point of mental exhaustion, nodded. The car that was to take us away from this gloomy place had been waiting for a while, its headlights shining invitingly. The Professor gave instructions for the baggage to be unloaded from the horses and into the car. That led to a new outburst of wrangling. The horse-man thought we were trying to slip away without paying. I tried to find my rock, but to no avail.

On the basis of Hobhouse's account, I had different expectations of this village: 'Not to alarm anyone with another adventure, we were all housed by seven o'clock in the evening, having been five hours coming from Libokavo – a distance of not more than nine miles. At coming in to the village, we were agreeably surprised by getting to a neat comfortable cottage, where we were received with a hearty welcome by the Albanian landlord, who, it turned out, was personally acquainted with the Signor Secretary. The name of the village was Cesarades, inhabited, except a few houses, by Christians. in this place every thing was on a different footing from what it had been in the Greek villages. We experienced a great deal of kindness and attention from our host; [...] It might certainly be called comfortable; and in it we passed a better night than any since our departure from Ioannina.'

The battle seemed to go on without end. It was like some force of nature against which mere humans were powerless to act.

'Let's just leave.' My voice was hardly audible above the racket. Demonstratively, I opened one of the car doors.

'Yes,' Karagjozi sighed, extracting himself from the tangle of people. 'Let's go.'

'Where will he sleep tonight?' I pointed to our tormentor.

Karagjozi shrugged his shoulders. 'He'll be alright.'

The car jerked into movement and we moved off, the horse-man in hot pursuit. His desperate face was illuminated in the red glow of the rear lights. He was completely confused.

I was overcome by a troublesome and misplaced sentiment: sympathy. 'Wait... wait a minute...', I signalled to the driver. He stopped and I wound down the window. The distraught head of our pursuer immediately appeared in the opening. I grasped his hand. 'Tomorrow!' I said. 'We'll be back tomorrow!' Not knowing what else to do, I took out a dollar bill to make it clear that he would be paid for his services. 'Tomorrow!' He calmed down a little. The driver put his foot on the gas and we disappeared into the night, along a sandy path full of potholes. The policemen were in the front, with the three of us sitting in the back in silence. My mind was empty. I had become waiting personified, waiting for this day to end. We drove through villages cloaked in darkness, the headlights illuminating groups of men sitting in front of houses. In a wide curve, we crossed the valley again, cutting straight through a dry river bed.

Somewhere near the end of days, we finally drove into Gjirokastër. One of the policemen knew a good hotel. 'It had better be cheap,' said Daniël. 'I'm not in the mood to be cheated. They seem to think here that all foreigners are rolling in money.'

Driven to distraction by fantasies of comfortable beds and foaming bathtubs, I was silently prepared to pay any price. We stopped at a promising modern hotel with a brightly lit restaurant.

How welcoming electric lights can be! Someone got out to ask the price, and was back in a trice. Full up, he said. How much can one person take in one day? More than you would think – it just went on and on.

'Listen,' said Karagjozi. 'I have a cousin here, a widow, who lives in a very nice house with a splendid bathroom – a Western European bathroom. Shall I call her?'

'I don't want to impose on anyone,' I said, with little conviction.

Dismissing my objections, Karagjozi got out of the car to find a telephone. Daniël and I waited, apathetic and silent, desensitised by the events of the day. Before long, the Professor returned. His brisk pace betrayed the good news. He must have secret reserves of energy. Yes, we could stay the night at his cousin's house.

'It was a strange city, and seemed to have been cast up in the valley one winter's night like some prehistoric creature that was now clawing its way up the mountainside. Everything in the city was old and made of stone, from the streets and fountains to the roofs of the sprawling age-old houses covered with grey slates like gigantic scales. It was hard to believe that, under this powerful carapace, the tender flesh of life survived and reproduced.

The traveller seeing it for the first time was tempted to compare it to something, but soon found that impossible, for the city rejected all comparisons.' This is how Ismail Kadare, the most famous Albanian writer, described his birthplace in the novel *Chronicle in Stone*.

We drove upwards over steep, cobbled streets between houses built closely together. The car manoeuvred into a side street and stopped – we would have to walk the rest of the way. The cousin was waiting for us, dressed in black, friendly, resigned and very pale. We entered an impeccable urban house. When we arrived in the living room, the television was switched on. Here, too, as in the house of the mayor of Libohovë, the room was dominated by an enormous wall unit, in which cups and glasses were arranged with mathematical precision, equidistant from each other. The walls were bare, with the exception of a picture of a grandchild. In the middle of the ceiling hung a lamp that emitted a clinical white light, making the widow even paler.

Karagjozi and Daniël ate an improvised warm meal, their plates on their laps. Doing penance for my greed of the previous evening, I had asked only for bread. The widow watched, her hands clasped together. It was up to me, I felt, to ask about the family.

Had her husband died long ago?

'Two years,' she nodded sadly.

Did she have any children?

Hefty photo albums were laid on my lap, full of pictures of her daughter's wedding, also showing her dear departed husband. Karagjozi excused himself and went to the bathroom. I was nearly falling off the sofa from exhaustion. My problem is that I remain friendly and interested until I drop dead. When rigor mortis sets in, I will continue to smile politely. Why was Karagjozi taking so long?

The eldest son came home. After greeting us curtly, he plonked himself down on the sofa, grabbed the remote control and started zapping through the channels. He was a modern youth, the opposite of the Albanians we had met on the mountain paths and whose interest in our welfare knew no bounds.

Finally, it was my turn, in the bathroom the sons had given their mother, the Professor had told me, to comfort her on the loss of her husband. 'It is a unique bathroom for Albania,' he told me. 'I will never be able to afford anything like it in my whole life.'

It was a small room, but the fittings were definitely of a quality not normally found in Albania. There was only enough room for a hip bath. I wriggled into it. Ah, what a relief for my stomach. I sat there for a while, my knees up to my chin, pondering the vulnerability of the human body. How often had I not cursed the 20th century and longed for a more primitive past that seemed to me more colourful and authentic? But now here I sat, surrounded by warm steam, full of gratitude for the four-wheeled motorised vehicle that had brought us back through a river bed to these modern comforts. I was, of course, a deserter. I had run away from my own journey, and from yours. I soothed my conscience by assuring myself that, if you had been able, you would certainly also have gone to Gjirokastër. Hobhouse expressed his disappointment that this was not possible: '[...] but I regret that the state of the country, and our situation as friends of Ali, did not permit us to visit the city, and obtain personal knowledge of the fact.'

Hobhouse described the situation he referred to a little earlier: 'Of Argyro-castro, which is very visible about nine miles to the north-west on the opposite hills, I learnt that it is a city supposed to contain twenty thousand inhabitants, chiefly Turks, being the capital of a Pashalik of two tails, and of a very populous district, bounding the east and north-east the country of the Chimeriotes. It was not, when we were in the country, in subjection to Ali, but nominally under the power of Ibrahim, Pasha of Vallona, the Prince with whom Ali was then at war, ...'

# Chapter 11

I WAS IN GOOD COMPANY with my stomach problems. In Patras, Byron also suffered terrible indigestion. The enemas and emetics he took on the advice of a doctor recommended by the British consul proved nearly fatal. He wrote to his sister Augusta that he had ultimately cured himself with a diet of rice and vinegar.

That put my own diet of mountain tea and a little bread in a different light. Bryon was used to long periods of fasting since his youth, mainly to combat his tendency to corpulence. At the age of 18, although only five feet eight inches, he weighed 202 pounds. Elisabeth Pigot, a close friend of the young Byron, called him a 'fat, bashful boy'.

Gabriël Matzneff describes with shrewdness and wit, yet with an undertone of admiration, how Byron's silhouette continually expanded and contracted throughout the 36 years of his life: 'To be attractive to those of his same age and to himself, to be able to move more easily, and to transform his body, Byron declared war on his obesity, by taking hot baths, boxing, fencing and, especially, swimming and horse-riding, two sports that enabled him to forget his deformity, – and finally by adopting an extremely rigorous diet that he continually observed – except when he had an attack of euphoria or fear – with unrelenting persistence and vigilance.'

Proudly, he kept his old schoolmates up to date on his progress, writing to them: 'You will not recognise me!' In only a few months, he lost more than 65 pounds, so much that many people no longer knew him, including the choirboy John Edleston, whose opinion he probably valued the most at that time. To one of his friends he wrote, in an early example of vain attention to his appearance, that his black hair had acquired a chestnut-brown gloss.

When he returned from his first Grand Tour in 1811 he wrote to his mother that he had become a vegetarian: that he now ate only green vegetables, potatoes and biscuits, and had given up drinking wine. Shortly after the publication of *Childe Harold*, a dinner was arranged to reconcile him with the poet Thomas Moore, who Byron had not spared in *English Bards and Scottish Reviewers*. Byron embarrassed everybody by insisting on being served nothing but hard biscuits and soda water, the only thing they did not have in the house. In the end, he settled for potatoes flattened and soaked in vinegar.

Later in life, he remained attracted to a Spartan daily routine: in the mornings a cup of strong green tea without milk or sugar and a raw beaten egg; in the middle of the day a few biscuits; and in the evening, vegetables with – this he allowed himself – two bottles of Bordeaux. Meat, he said, was 'for boxers'.

But he would not be the man of contradictions that he was if this self-imposed discipline had not compelled him to do exactly the opposite from time to time. In 1814 he wrote to his now close friend Thomas Moore – not without a little self-mockery – that, as a vegetarian, he had set himself the goal of eating meat only when others did not: '... the other day I nearly killed myself with a collar of brawn. [...] All this gourmandise was in honour of Lent.'

During the first two years of his stay in Venice, from 1816 to 1818, he not only indulged excessively in sensual pleasures (his lovers passed each other on the steps of his house), but also in food and drink.

An English visitor observed: 'Lord Byron could not have been more than 30, but he looked 40. His face had become pale, bloated and sallow. He had grown very fat, his shoulders broad and round, and the knuckles of his hands were lost in fat.' Thomas Moore, who visited him during that period, was more subtle in his remarks: 'He had grown fatter both in person and face, and the latter had most suffered by the change, having lost, by the enlargement of the features, some of that refined and spiritualised look that had, in other times, distinguished it.' But he added: 'He was still, however, eminently handsome; and, in exchange for whatever his features might have lost of their high, romantic character, they had become more fitted for the expression of that arch, waggish wisdom, that Epicurean play of humour...'.

A few years later his somewhat longer-lasting love affair with Countess Teresa Guiccioli motivated him to fast again. Shelley, who met Byron regularly, wrote to his wife Mary in 1821: 'He has in fact completely recovered his health & lives a life totally the reverse of that which he led in Venice.' When a certain Lady Blessington, who he met in Genoa, advised him to follow a more nutritious regimen, he replied that 'if he did, he should get fat and stupid, and that it was only by abstinence that he felt he had the power of exercising his mind'. He was thus not driven only by vanity, but also by the conviction that the power of his mind and his intelligence suffered when he was overweight.

Byron's diets did not include a self-imposed ban on alcoholic drink: 'To be sure, I drink two bottles of wine at dinner,' he admits, 'but they form only a vegetable diet.' In 1814 he wrote to Thomas Moore: ' I have also been drinking, and, on one occasion, with three other friends at the Cocoa Tree, from six till four, yea, unto five in the matin. We clareted and champagned till two – then supped, and finished with a kind of regency punch composed of madeira, brandy and green tea, no real water being admitted therein [...]. And so, – I am very well, and they say it will hurt my constitution.'

According to Thomas Medwin, a cousin of Shelley's, while in Italy Byron drank a concoction of alcoholic drink and water as a cure for kidney stones, a complaint he had suffered in 1812. Byron liked to tease Medwin: 'Why don't you drink, Medwin? Gin-and-water is the source of all my inspiration. If you were to drink as much as I do, you would write as good verses; depend on it, it is the Hippocrene.'

Drink as muse and self-medication. Perhaps the drink allayed the hunger. Byron also chewed tobacco and smoked a pipe to the same effect. He preferred to eat alone, beyond reach of comment on his diet. Sometimes, the determination with which he refrained from eating took on anorexic proportions. In 1813 he wrote in his journal: 'I wish I could leave off eating altogether.' There was contempt for food in his almost creed-like statement: '[...] and I will not be the slave of my appetite.'

He would not allow women to drink anything other than champagne in his presence and eat anything other than lobster salad, while he himself got headaches from champagne. He suffered from an exceptional thirst. He could drink 15 bottles of soda water in an evening, claiming that he did not even take the time to uncork them, simply breaking the neck of the bottle.

His extreme eating habits were driven not only by a hatred of obesity and the fear of dulling his creative capacities, but also by his hypochondria. He often felt unwell, and sounded the alarm at the slightest tinge or pain. He never travelled without a doctor and always had an impressive stock of pills and potions with him. He was also addicted to laudanum, a painkiller and tranquiliser. Even as a student at Cambridge, two years before his Grand Tour, he wrote to a friend that he kept himself going when writing his poetry with medicinal drinks and women: 'The two last amusements have not had the best effect in the world; for my attentions have been divided amongst so many fair damsels, and the drugs I swallow are of such variety in their composition, that between Venus and Aesculapius I am harassed to death.'

He must have had an iron constitution. He could swim for hours in waters notorious for their currents, and he could ride endlessly. In love, he was insatiable, especially during his years in Venice. He was a night owl. When he had the urge to write he could be extremely productive in a very short time, especially at night. Everything suggests that he was a sanguine individual, with a lust for life which – as the years progressed – was increasingly tempered by an equally strong *taedium vitae*, deep despondency, unbearable ennui. In this way, he swung constantly between euphoria and melancholy.

It is not surprising that his body followed this up and down pattern. With his diets and medicines, intended to maintain the quality of his life at a high level, he made himself ill – perhaps unconsciously pandering to his world-weariness. He developed chronic indigestion – no wonder, given a daily regime that contained so much yeast and carbon dioxide and so little nutritious ingredients. Doctors who conducted an autopsy after he died at the age of 36 concluded that he had the bones of an 80-year-old. It was what we now know as osteoporosis, caused by a severe lack of calcium and other minerals. The diagnosis was that he had lived life to the full, and those around him shuddered in admiration.

# Chapter 12

DEAR FRIEND, AN archaic sound – clip clop, clip clop – penetrated my sleep. The horse-man! I shot upright, crossed the room and opened the window. Below was a narrow street, paved with stone in a grey and white striped pattern. A line of pack-animals was moving slowly along it. With their heads bowed, they trotted lazily up the hill. Two of them had riders on their backs, who allowed themselves to be carried along so sluggishly, dreaming with their eyes open, that they looked as though they could drop off to sleep at any moment.

A little further down, on a flat roof, a woman in a button-up pinafore dress of the kind that are so common in southern Europe, was shearing the wool from a sheepskin. She was so intent on her work, she saw and heard nothing. As I looked down at the landscape of roofs covered in flat stones of all shades of pink, grey and sandy brown, a passage from *Chronicle in Stone* came into my mind: '... it was surely the only place in the world where, if you slipped and fell in the street, you might well land on the roof of a house.' And: 'In some places you could walk down the street, and hang your hat on a minaret.'

We had breakfast in the living room, under the portrait of the grandchild. I felt refreshed and content that fate had brought us to Gjirokastër, the birthplace of Enver Hoxha, Ismail Kadare and Afrim Karagjozi. The Professor was born here in 1941, into a family that originally came from Souli. His grandfather had been a large landowner. Enormous flocks of sheep grazed his land and he lived in one of the largest houses in Gjirokastër.

'A family that produced patriots and intellectuals,' said Karagjozi, his chest swelling while, at the same time, the furrow on his brow deepened.

At the time of Ali Pasha, two Karagjozi brothers had been the elders of the family. Ali called one of them Topi, the Great Cannon, because of his bravery. Proud of this self-earned epithet, the brother used it for his whole branch of the family. The Topullis would produce a series of courageous warriors, including Cerçiz and Bajo Topulli, who led an uprising against the Turks in 1908.

Quemal Karagjozi, Afrim's father, was born in 1912. He attended the French lyceum in Korça and, at the age of 20, went to Paris to study at the Sorbonne. He soon became a member of the Albanian Patriotic Society, which comprised mainly students and workers. Seven years later he returned to his fatherland, because it had been occupied by the Italians. He immediately joined the Movement for the Liberation of Albania, and became one of the most prominent local leaders of the Communist Party, which was active in the resistance. He seemed to have everything going for him: he was well educated, possessed wide cultural knowledge, spoke fluent French, German and Italian, and was a gifted orator. And he was an idealist *par excellence*: he dreamed of an Albania that was 'prosperous for everyone'.

When the Professor came to this point in his father's story, his face, which had been aglow with reverence and affection, became tense. 'He never knew why,' he said. 'But in 1943 he was suddenly expelled from the party.'

His father may have been a friend of Hoxha, who was four years his junior, but Hoxha had no qualms about liquidating friends and party colleagues so that he could be 'the one and only'. He did not tolerate capable people around him, seeing them only as a potential threat.

As with many Albanians in this tumultuous period, a shadow fell over the life of Quemal Karagjozi. The ancestral home was destroyed during a bomb attack in 1942 because the Communists often held meetings there. After the war ended, he was unemployed and the family moved to Tirana, where there was more chance of finding work. Eventually, because of a heart complaint, he was declared unfit to work and had to support his family on a minimal pension. For the rest of his life, he bore the burden of his unjust and incomprehensible suspension from the Party, unaware that arbitrariness and an apparent absence of logic not only typified Hoxha's regime but were inherent to the system in all Communist countries.

'And yet he remained an optimist,' says the Professor with a sigh. 'He always said that, one day, something good would happen to Albania.'

Gjirokastër is much older than the 14th-century Byzantine records in which it is first mentioned. Perhaps the name has an etymological connection with the Argyris, an Illyrian tribe. The oldest part is a robust citadel on a protruding rock, high above the city. A wide variety of flags have flown from the tower. After the end of Byzantine rule, the Turkish flag hung over the castle for five centuries. If you had travelled through this area two years later, you would have been able to visit the city, as in 1811, after a long siege, it finally fell to Ali Pasha. I was unable to discover what fate befell Ibrahim Pasha – history has less to say about losers.

Kadare tells us: 'It was not easy to be a child in that city.' Through the eyes of this child, a small boy at the outbreak of the Second World War, the reader sees how the Italians, and then the Germans take control of Gjirokastër: 'The Italians came back to the city. In the morning the road was filled with mules, guns and endless columns of soldiers. [...] The siren, the searchlight, the anti-aircraft battery, the nuns and the prostitutes all followed the soldiers in.' And some years later: 'At dusk, the city, which through the centuries had appeared on maps as a possession of the Romans, the Normans, the Byzantines, the Turks, the Greeks and the Italians now watched darkness fall as a part of the German empire. Utterly exhausted, dazed by the battle, it showed no sign of life.'

The city's inhabitants themselves were divided. At the end of the war, young partisans took justice into their own hands and executed monarchists and nationalists, including old comrades-in-arms who were vaguely suspected of having such sympathies.

After breakfast we walked through 'the city of a thousand steps' in search of a dispensary and to change some dollars. Everywhere there were improvised market stalls. Anyone who had anything to sell set their wares out on a cloth or a folding table and waited for customers. They were like still lifes by Jopie Huisman: a pair of worn shoes on a stained cloth, a clock with no workings, indeterminate items of clothing of equally indeterminate origin – the amateur beginnings of a free-market economy. Somewhere on a stone step sat a woman whose mouth was pulled into such a grimace of desperation that I bought a bunch of bananas from her. It was the only fruit she was selling while, not far from the city, I had seen trees full of pomegranates and vegetable gardens with overripe melons and pumpkins begging to be picked. Her decoratively arranged assortment comprised a chaotic range of articles, including chewing gum, soap, fruit juice and washing powder. Perhaps she dreamed of owning a well-stocked supermarket and her despair grew out of the unbridgeable gap between dream and reality.

Karagjozi did the talking in the dispensary, pointing sideways in the general direction of my tormented stomach. Interested, the sales assistant looked at my stomach, muttered a diagnosis and gave me a strip of indefinable pills, one of which I took without even thinking. Now the dollars. We had been advised to exchange money on the free market, but since none of us knew the exchange rate, we decided to look for a bank. Around us I saw many young people in jeans, the sacred and ubiquitous uniform of youth. The further east you go in Europe, the closer you come to the graves of Stalin, Ceausescu or Hoxha, the more denim dominates the scene on the streets. East meets West, in the form of (imitation) Levis. Suddenly, I was holding a handful of *lekë*, some bearing the esteemed head of Ismail Qemali, the leader of the first popular democratic government in Albania in 1912. And on each banknote, of course, was the eagle with the two heads.

At the house of Karagjozi's cousin, the policemen from the previous evening were waiting for us. We only knew each other as dark shadows. Now we could see each other properly, so we introduced ourselves. They were Roberto and Hadji. They had brought a Volkswagen bus with a driver and it had been agreed that they would accompany us today – probably by the Professor to avoid the risk of a disaster for the third consecutive day.

We drove back to the disastrous Qesarat. The bus was fitted out like a living room, with openwork curtains on the sides and the windscreen decorated with a frill, dangling chains, and a plastic hand grasping a bundle of imitation banknotes. The strange polyphonic male voices emitting from the radio had a hypnotic effect as the bus ploughed along the riverbed like a ship on wheels.

'Shepherds' songs from the distant past,' said Karagjozi. 'The text reflects the human dilemmas of birth, marriage, death and the harvest. It is a speciality of this area, and the best singers come from Gjirokastër.'

The multi-vocal music, without accompaniment, was so terribly difficult that only those who started very young could learn it. Its most striking quality was that the vocal sequences ended abruptly, as though the narrator had been silenced in the middle of his tale, perhaps with a knife between his ribs, his mouth stuck open for eternity without ever uttering another sound – a victim, in the end, of a blood feud.

The bus bumped upwards over a wide path until, still a quarter of an hour from Qesarat, we caught sight of the horseman. Concerned that he would not get his money, he had come to meet us. Our feelings about him had somewhat tempered and we had decided, as there was no alternative, to keep him on – as long as we could reach a financial compromise and he behaved reasonably. Even the Professor, after a good night's sleep, seemed to show signs of leniency.

We got out of the bus and the Professor and the horseman sat down amiably next to each other on the grass. The horseman, too, a blade of grass in his mouth, seemed calm and chastened. He seemed to have shaved his face and, without his stubble, created a much more civilised impression. He even took the trouble to explain everything in great detail. The owner of the horses asked 20 dollars a horse. It was up to us to decide what we paid him, but he would have to pay the 60 dollars a day, whatever happened.

'But that's absurd!' Daniël cried. 'A labourer earns eight dollars a day here, and a horse can earn 20?'

Roberto and Hadji agreed with him. Yes, it was too crazy for words. When the Professor translated Daniël's exclamation into Albanian, the horseman once again erupted into a rage. This was the horseman we had come to know, with rolling eyes and a red head – very reassuring. Once again, tempers flared, and Roberto joined the fray, his hawk's profile designed for attack. Daniël fielded one condemnation after the other in the direction of the horseman. 'The first day, he was completely useless, and yesterday, he got us all lost!'

I looked surreptitiously at my watch.

'It's already twelve o'clock,' I said. 'Before we know it, it will be one, or two. We have a long way to go and it gets dark at seven.'

'We have to negotiate,' Daniël replied.

'We've been doing that since yesterday evening! I'm prepared to pay whatever he wants, if we can leave now, with the horses.'

Daniël shook his head, full of disapproval: 'If you give them what they want, you ruin the market,' he said, 'They lose all sense of proportion.'

I saw the Professor grab his chest. The previous evening, before we had disappeared into our separate rooms, he had whispered to me in the semi-darkness: 'You know, the horseman... he threatened to strangle me.' These never-ending negotiations would be the death of him. Our aversion to the horseman increased by the minute. It overcame whatever remained of my pragmatic compliance. I looked wistfully at my blonde mare. Everyone wanted to be done with this born troublemaker. Now. Immediately.

I gave up. 'Let's give him half. Two hundred dollars for his services so far, and send him packing.'

Daniël shrugged his shoulders. He still found it far too much, but so be it. But the horseman did not agree. Now he really lost his head, gesticulating wildly in all directions, like a madman directing the traffic – his lips were foaming, threats and curses flew from his mouth like startled starlings.

We were dumbfounded. The man really was insane. I decided to pay him, whether he wanted to or not. And, when it came down to it, he did. He held out his hand and counted along with us, his eyes on stalks. At last, he held 20 banknotes, a stiff ransom, in his fist.

The driver stepped meaningfully on the gas, and we all scrambled to get back into the car as soon as we could. We took one last look at this one-man catastrophe, this master at creating confusion and dispute. He sat at the side of the road and lit a cigarette. He seemed to be staring ahead of him and growling softly.

'So,' said Karagjozi. 'We are back in control. That man has done a good job of ruining this trip for me.'

'Forget him,' I said, reminding him that travelling on horseback had also been a daily recurring nightmare for you and Hobhouse.

We discussed how we would rearrange the day without horses. The only alternative was to cover the distance we had planned on foot. We estimated it would take us about four hours to walk. Roberto and Hadji knew the way, and the bus could take the baggage as far as Erind, the second-to-last village. The driver agreed to do this, on the condition that the Professor would accompany him, to share responsibility for the safety of our rucksacks.

The Professor did not protest. I had the feeling the he and his heart badly needed a day's rest. In Erind, he said, he could use the time looking for horses for the last stage of the journey to Tepelene. According to Hobhouse, that had taken you seven hours.

'So what is a Vlach?' I asked Daniël.

'They are a people who, according to a Romanian theory, originally come from Wallachia,' he said. 'It is now part of Romania – the Vlach language is reputed to be a Romanian dialect. But the Greeks claim that they are natives who – under the influence of the Romans and unaware of it themselves – starting speaking a Latin dialect, related to that spoken by the Romanians. In the distant past, the Vlachs were herders and caravan drivers, and became dispersed, especially around Metsovo in the Pindus mountains, and South Albania. Their language is threatened with extinction, because it is not taught in schools and there is increasing intermarriage with non-Vlachs. They are not as dark as the Greeks, often have blue eyes, lighter hair and square faces.'

'Why do you think our horse-man is a Vlach?'

'Because he looks like one.'

I tried in vain to remember the colour of the horseman's eyes, but could only recall their glare. They could suddenly flash, unpredictably and arbitrarily, and whoever he happened to be looking at fell prey to a strange mixture of confusion, fear and rage.

In Qesarat, a boy filled my canteen from the village well. It was cloudy but dry, and the unnamed medicine had done its work. The journey resumed, with a change of personnel. Roberto was the prototype Albanian that I had seen in prints and photos: slightly built, with bronzed skin, black eyes and eyebrows, and a curved nose in a narrow, finely drawn face. In his uniform, he looked like your friendly neighbourhood policeman, but in the classical garb of a robber and with a knife between his teeth, I would not have had the courage to hire him as a dragoman. Hadji, who was more heavily built, had a boxer's nose and, in profile, looked like a little Jean-Paul Belmondo.

While Daniël and Roberto – who proved to speak reasonable Greek – walked on ahead, and were sometimes hidden from sight behind a bend in the mountain path or a bunch of trees, Hadji stuck close to my side. He was not content to communicate only in sign language. He pointed at the nearest mountain and said emphatically: 'Mali'. 'Mali', I repeated. 'Roege', he continued, pointing at the path. 'Kokí – head. Kaputzet – foot.' Keeping time with our pace, we repeated words. When I could repeat them without mistake, he would say: 'Hrodone', which meant OK. Albania was not Albania, but Shqiperia – I had to make sure I remembered that. And, at last, I had found someone who knew the names of the trees and plants. Hadji took a childish pleasure in naming everything that his eyes beheld in field and meadow – our walk became a wondrous demonstration of language and symbol.

Our path still ran along the flanks of the Lunxheris mountains, with the valley of the Drino to our left. The further we progressed, the more I found myself having to leave behind images that I wanted to burn on my retina forever. There was no need to have taken water with us. It was there for the taking, in clear streams that had cut their way through capricious rocks formations and dark caverns in which the Oreads live, mountain nymphs who guide travellers safely over the rocks. Bent over forwards, my hands cupped to drink the clear water, I silently asked for their assistance, though in Hadji I already had an excellent mountain nymph. Our dragomen had unbuttoned their uniform jackets, but still wore their caps, with their red braid and gold badge, to save carrying them.

One of Roberto's cousins lived in the first village we came to, Dhoksat. On a whim, he suggested we go and visit her. Why not? After the disaster of the previous day, we were in an exuberant mood. Nothing else could happen to us, and we had plenty of time. Passing through a tidy garden that struck a strange contrast to the wildness of the surroundings, we entered an old, but well-maintained house. We took off our shoes and left them at the entrance, as though we were entering a mosque. I took a quick look at my socks to see if there were any holes in them. I can never be bothered to darn socks, but think it a waste to throw them away just because they have a hole in – behold the dilemma of a Western woman at the end of the 20th century. Luckily, I had no reason to be embarrassed about the pair I was wearing.

We entered a room with a low ceiling and sat down on one of the sofas against the wall. Curious, giggling girls jostled in the doorway to look at us. Roberto's cousin, one of those women who are plump and eternally cheerful, came and shook our hands. Two of her daughters, 12 and 14 years old, could speak a little English and were pushed reluctantly in our direction. The eldest had a classical face, framed with black curls, while the younger one bore a striking resemblance to the cracked portrait of her mother that hung above the sofa, which the mother herself no longer did. The eldest told us, constructing her sentences carefully, that she later wanted to leave Albania. For Italy. She beamed just at the thought.

Our hostess brought us drinks, coffee and raki for the men, mountain tea for me. She then returned to her domain and left her shy daughters to talk to the guests. A little later, her husband came home. With his heavy-framed, Sartre-style glasses he looked like a thoughtful, introvert intellectual. He was a history teacher – though where, in this remote place, was a mystery.

We talked about you. He seemed to consider our mission uninteresting and unnecessary. He was most likely one of these historians who believe that the past should be studied from behind a desk and not relived. He frowned and drew our attention to another hero, a real one, from Albanian history. He rose from his chair and removed a book from the shelf with which he hoped to impress his Dutch colleague. But because he spoke only Albanian, and Roberto translated his words into poor Greek, he was unable to inspire Daniël with his enthusiasm.

Exhausted from all the linguistic confusion, we left. The raki had had its effect and my companions were even more exuberant than before. I took a picture of a man leading a donkey loaded down with twigs. In the background, you can see Roberto and Daniël laughing hysterically. Roberto was having such fun, he nearly tumbled over the edge into the gorge.

As we approached the next village, which according to the map, was called Qestorat, we saw a couple on the side of the road picking fruit the size of cherries from a tree. They were striking because they were both blond, which is exceptional in this region, and the three children who were playing around the base of the tree were just as fair as their parents. They gave us some fruit to taste. It was nearly all stone, and seemed hardly worth taking the trouble to pick. The couple immediately stopped working and insisted that we drink something with them.

'It would be impolite to refuse,' said Roberto, his eyes twinkling at the thought of more raki.

The family led us through winding streets. We crossed a bare square, bordered by empty houses that must once have belonged to wealthy citizens. The denunciation of the bourgeoisie was also a declaration of war against beauty, style and elegance. The family house was opposite a Byzantine church that seemed to be still in use. We ascended a staircase to the first floor and entered a living room dominated by the most hideous wall tapestry that I have ever seen. It depicted a fleeing stag, in thick black contours and bright, clashing colours. It was probably the family's *pièce de résistance*.

The table was laid with cola, beer, raki, lemonade, biscuits, nuts and Turkish delight. They were very disappointed that I only wanted mountain tea. I pointed to my stomach. Ah, *stomaaki*! The family looked at me with concern. They thought it even stranger that I did not want sugar in the tea. The inhabitants of this region clearly had a very sweet tooth – perhaps a legacy of the Turkish occupation. I had never seen so many people with bad teeth, including the children.

It started to get crowded in the room. The neighbour came by with his wife, who was carrying a pale baby in her arms. Then grandma joined the fray. She hugged me tightly, as though I were her long-lost daughter. It was possible – I looked very much like her daughter, who kept smiling at me in wonder and did her utmost to make me feel at home. In other times, in another life, I could have been her sister.

They wanted to know all about us. How old was Daniël? How old was I? Were we married? How many children did we have? When they heard how old I was, they were amazed at my teeth – were they all mine? How could that be? Good dentists in Holland, Daniël explained, matter-of-factly. The neighbour's baby was placed on my lap, and I kept myself occupied talking to him in a language that babies all around the world understand and appreciate, especially when you tickle their tummies. For the first time, the women stayed with us. Was that because this was a family with Christian roots? I thought of Hobhouse, who sometimes made reference to villages where the majority of inhabitants were Christians.

More beer was placed on the table. Roberto was so exuberant that there were sparks flying off him. What were we to do later with a drunk dragoman? Perhaps Daniël was secretly asking himself the same question. He unfolded the map and he and our host started to look at the route we still had to complete.

I slipped away to look at the church. The woman with the baby was walking along behind me. She nodded to me: the door was always open. Once I became accustomed to the semi-darkness I saw that the walls were crowded with frescos. From a domed ceiling, the 12 apostles stood looking down on us in a ring, surrounded by depictions of biblical scenes. Another Daniël stood in the lion's den, his hands raised to heaven a little too elegantly. Without a word, they told their stories, creating an emphatic silence. But if you closed your eyes, you could hear the rustle of the finely chiselled wings of the angels. On both sides of the altar was a wooden panel showing shells and flowers in vases. Here and there, a broken carnation lay on a ledge. Generations of oil lamps and candles had left trails of grease and wax. On the altar itself, there were freshly picked flowers, and at the back was a pitifully empty tabernacle from which the Holy of Holies had long ago been stolen.

I heard shuffling and turned round. A woman in black, a head-scarf tied tightly around her head, was leaning on a stick and looking at me with empty eyes. One of Michelangelo's Fates. Was she the village elder, the ancestral mother of Qestorat? Did she date back to Byzantium, and had survived the Turks and the Communists? When we left the church, she disappeared between the moss-covered tomb-stones of the adjoining graveyard, or perhaps there was a grave some-where that she could step in and out of as she pleased.

In the house, I found the whole group just as I had left it. But in the next village, there was a professor waiting for us, most likely with a deep furrow across his barrow. We had to move on.

Happily tipsy, the men left the premises. We were given an elabo-rate send-off. Grandmother hugged me to her breast and my imagi-nary sister ran after me with two bunches of mountain tea, for my *stomaaki*. Watched by the villagers, we continued on our way. From a roof terrace, between Dionysian bunches of purple-blue grapes, two little cupids with chubby cheeks looked down on us. In the gateway of an old and robust stone house, a woman of my age was standing. Although she did not yet have a single wrinkle in her face, her spine had been affected by a form of arthritis, which made her body bend increasingly forward. Without medical treatment, the process would continue until her nose touched the ground. Such crooked beings are depicted on Roman vases and reliefs. You could say that the affliction had always been around, and was sufficiently revered to be immortal-ised. That is of course no comfort, just a reminder of the plagues that can strike all those who walk the earth, and are of all ages.

There was an enormous nut-tree along the side of the road. A tree so thick that it takes four people to embrace it inspires me with as much awe as a cathedral. But not everything grew and flowered here with so much ease. I also saw neglected vineyards, where weeds were shooting up between knotty stumps with half-withered foliage. I felt it was a bad sign if a country could not maintain its vineyards – it had lost its esprit.

We reached the village of Mingul-Nokove. On an unpaved square, the villagers were standing around chatting and watching a game of football. Was this one of those villages where everyone met each other spontaneously? Without checking their diaries? Had this country, despite being afflicted by all possible forms of terrors, perhaps managed to preserve more of life 'as it is supposed to be' than we had in the West?

You and your entourage arrived in Erind around half past three – we got there three hours later. But you didn't make any visits en route, or drink beer and raki. The sun had already set, but had left behind a hazy, pink atmosphere that made the village look warm and welcoming. In a vegetable garden, where giant pumpkins seemed to have fallen from space, a woman was working, against a backdrop of haystacks and blue mountains. On a small hillock alongside the road, grandfathers, sons and grandsons were sitting together. I would never know what they were talking about – or were they content to sit together in silence? Photo, photo... they called to us, so I took a picture. As when I took a picture of the footballers on the square, I again felt a sense of melancholy. Who am I, where do I come from, where am I going? Would they ever ask themselves these questions?

When I developed the photograph later, they all looked good-natured and relaxed. Standing, squatting... What do you do in Albania if someone points a camera at you? You put your arms around your neighbour's shoulders.

After the photo opportunity we were followed by a continually swelling horde of children, all wearing the kind of plastic sandals that, nearly 50 years previously, my father had made me wear at the seaside in case I stepped on any pieces of glass or sharp shells. We were as much of a curiosity to them, as they to us. 'We're Martians,' said Daniël, laconically striding forth. A little farther on, the children's great-grandfathers were sitting on a low wall, their caps on and their rosaries between their fingers.

And there, too, was Afrim Karagjozi. He came towards us, asking in a concerned voice: 'Are you alright?' Better than ever, we told him. It had been a fantastic trip, a shame that he had not been there. He admitted that it had been a little dull for him, after the driver had left. But, he had found another horseman.

We spent the night in the village at the home of a retired couple, who had both been teachers. 'We were comfortably lodged,' as Hobhouse would have said. The husband was a tall, handsome man. His wife had a worried look on her face and scuttled back and forth as though our visit demanded the utmost of her powers of improvisation.

When we arrived I wanted to freshen up and change my clothes. Now that the sun had set it was suddenly cold. I asked for the toilet. The wife indicated to me to follow her outside. We crossed a muddy yard. She kept turning round to make sure I was following her. Shyly, she pointed to a small shed at the back of the garden, next to the chicken run. I nodded and opened the squeaky door. It was a squat toilet, yes, and indescribably filthy. I had only seen something like this once before, in the Dordogne, about 30 years previously. There was an impossibly white pedal bin in a corner and when you squatted over the hole, trying desperately to keep your balance, there was a roll of toilet paper hanging at eye level. I didn't know where to put my feet. I tried to ignore the all-permeating stench of human excrement, and of chicken dung from next door. I resolved to read Hobhouse again to find out how these things were arranged in your time. The teacher was clearly not a handyman, or he would have hammered together a half decent toilet by now. When I went back outside, the wife was waiting for me, the same worried look on her face. She indicated that I should wash my hands and pointed to a tap in an outer wall, with a plastic bowl underneath it – the basin and sink of the house. I held my hands under the hesitant trickle, while she stood next to me with a solemn face and a crispy clean towel over her arm. It would have been pure slapstick, if had not been so endearing.

We went inside. I pulled on a thick jumper and summoned up the courage to ask if I could wash two items of clothing. So we went back outside, to fill a tub with water. We stood for at least ten minutes staring in polite silence as the water once again trickled reluctantly out of the tap, occasionally looking at each other by accident and smiling. Without Karagjozi, we couldn't say a word to each other. At some point, she disappeared and came back with a packet of washing powder. I washed my clothes and hung them on a line between two orange trees.

I went back into the living room. Roberto and Hadji, accompanied by the driver from Gjirokastër, had been served with more drinks. The new horseman had arrived to introduce himself. He was small and tawny, and his wrinkles were in the right places to give him a smile that had etched itself out around his mouth and eyes. While the Professor recounted our experiences with the first horseman, our host came and listened, amused. His wife asked what we would like to eat. I told her why I had been fasting for two days. She advised me to try boiled potatoes and a boiled egg, provoking a discussion among all those present about which was better for the stomach: a hard or a soft-boiled egg.

Some were thoroughly convinced that hard-boiled is better, because it would eliminate all bacteria, while others were equally convinced that a soft-boiled egg was easier to digest. The company divided into two camps, like the Small-Endians and the Big-Endians in *Gulliver's Travels*, who were at war over whether a boiled egg should be opened at the small (pointed) end or the big end. After much debate, we agreed on a 'medium' as a compromise and the wife disappeared into a room under the stairs to cook the meal. If only all Balkan disputes could be settled so easily, it would save a lot of grief and UN peace troops.

Now the negotiations started on the horses for the next day. Our man had one horse of his own, the others he had to rent from someone in the village. He asked 30 dollars a horse. Karagjozi nearly fell off the sofa in amazement. The horseman explained that, normally speaking, a working horse would earn 30 dollars a day. Roberto and Hadji grinned, the discussion that ensued sounded familiar. Again the same argument: surely a horse can't earn more in a day than a university professor! The new horseman did not get angry. He listened attentively, understanding that this was a reasonable argument. How lucky we are, I thought, that car hire companies have tables with fixed rates. Just imagine having to haggle endlessly like this every time we wanted to rent a car.

The horseman was prepared to compromise. The Professor too, in that way they reached an agreement that everyone was happy with. It was also decided that we would only go as far as the bridge over the Drino on horseback. On the other side, the original path to Tepelene was hidden underneath an 11-kilometer long highway. Our driver from Gjirokastër would wait for us at the bridge with his living room on wheels. We raised our glasses to seal the deal, and our cheerful mood returned.

We said emotional farewells to our dragomen, who were going back to the City of Stone. Roberto would accompany us again the following day. The table was laid with dishes of feta, boiled eggs, meat and steaming potatoes. After all the mountain tea, I was starving, but the Professor was engaged in an animated conversation with the teacher and didn't show the slightest interest in what was on the table. The wife remained invisible for the time being. Was she waiting politely for the conversation to end, or was she observing a practice that I had read about in an account by a 19th-century English traveller? When he was finally able to eat lobster in Greece, the hostess first let everything go cold because 'it was better for the stomach'.

As if someone had given an invisible sign, the conversation came to an end and we started to eat. 'Is your wife not eating with us?' I asked. 'Yes, yes...' The teacher nodded indifferently. She did not join us, unnoticed, until halfway through the meal. A plate of potatoes has never tasted so good and the egg, well it was indeed the perfect compromise. Karagjozi, inspired by the way I cut the egg into small pieces and was clearly enjoying every small mouthful, told us that after his father was fired, they were so poor that they could only afford one egg for the whole family at Easter. His mother boiled it and carefully cut it into three, garnishing it with whatever they had in the house. It was served up like caviar. *Nouvelle cuisine avant la lettre*, but born of a great sorrow.

Thinking back on our journey I asked why the vineyards had been so neglected. The teacher said there were several reasons. The young people who could have breathed new life into the wine-making industry had all left to go abroad. And a lot of money was needed to buy machinery, pesticides, artificial fertiliser, vehicles, etc. Where was that to come from? Foreign investors were afraid to take the risk. The whole farming and fruit-growing sector had the same problem. On top of that many of the processing plants that used to be run by cooperatives under the Communists had been destroyed by their former workers as years of accumulated frustration finally erupted. Since then, many fields were left to run wild.

'This is a rich country,' sighed Karagjozi. 'But it needs to be exploited.'

He recalled nostalgically the early 1970s when, together with his secondary school pupils, he had helped build terraces on the mountainsides on the southwest coast of Albania, which were then planted with olive and orange trees. It was a compulsory national programme, part of Enver Hoxha's campaign to 'make the hills and mountains as fertile as the plains'. Now, said the Professor, all those trees were withering away, with no one to prune or harvest them.

We also learned why the wife wore such a sorrowful expression on her face: her three daughters lived in Greece with their husbands and children, she told us, because they could find work there and not here. The old family ties, which had long remained intact here in the mountains, were now being destroyed by the exodus of younger generations that was gathering momentum.

I went to bed feeling a little depressed. Gone was the exuberance of the afternoon, when I – with my background of Western prosperity – had shamelessly surrendered to a romanticised vision of life in the villages we passed through. Something of the desolation and the hopelessness of Albania had rubbed off on me. It was as though all attempts to progress in this country had failed – a circumstance which, given the country's history, had already persisted for too long, though each time in a different form. Anyone can be born in the wrong place at the wrong time. But in Albania, it seemed as though you were always born at the wrong time. That this country was 'abounding in more natural beauties than the classical regions of Greece' did nothing to change that. Food comes first, then the beauty of nature.

# Chapter 13

To walk from qesarat to erind, as we did, would have
been impossible for Lord Byron.

'Out, hunchback!'
'I was born so, mother!'

This is how the drama *The Deformed Transformed* begins. Two
revealing sentences that succinctly portray the relationship between
Byron, as a child, and his mother. If the emotional and unpredictable woman was in a bad temper, she would reproach him for his
handicap. He, in turn, would blame her for it for his entire life. He
was convinced that it was because she had worn a corset during her
pregnancy, or because she had been over-sensitive during the birth.

There are widely varying theories about the true nature of Byron's
disability. Did he really have a club foot? Was it a genetic deformity,
the consequence of infantile paralysis, or did something indeed go
wrong during his birth?

After Byron's death, his friend Edward Trelawney, the victim of his
own overactive imagination, tried to have the foot put on display in a
curiosity cabinet. While Byron's body was lying in an open coffin for
people to pay their last respects, he decided to inspect it and unravel
the secret once and for all. After sending Fletcher from the room
to fetch him a glass of water, Trelawney lifted the robe that covered
the corpse and discovered to his amazement that both his friend's
feet were clubbed, and the legs withered to the knee. 'The form and
features of an Apollo, with the feet and legs of a sylvan satyr,' wrote
Trelawney, in his hunger for sensation. And this from someone who
had been swimming with Byron on countless occasions!

Thomas Medwin, with whom Byron spent some time in Italy,

unintentionally gives a more credible description: 'I expected to discover that he had a club, perhaps a cloven foot; but it would have been difficult to have distinguished one from the other, either in size or in form.'

His mother herself clearly described what was wrong with him, when he had just started to walk. In a letter to his aunt Mrs Leigh, she asked for her help in purchasing a special shoe: 'George's foot turns inward, and it is the right foot; he walks quite on the side of his foot.'

In his first months at Harrow, too, his schoolmates teased him painfully about his deformity. Sometimes he would wake up to find that they had put his foot in a tub of water. He learned to fight to defend himself. At first he hated the school but, as time passed, he fought to establish a place for himself and made friends. A shoe had been designed for him with a strap around the ankle, but he was lazy and forgot to wear it. He wanted to do what the others did – and with enormous willpower engaged in a wide variety of sports, simply ignoring his handicap. When he was 11, a self-styled practitioner massaged his foot with oil and screwed it to a machine that was extremely painful and did no good at all. After that, a special 'orthopaedic boot' was made for him.

At the age of 15, his torment came from a different quarter. Byron had met his cousin Mary Chatworth, who lived on an estate not far from Newstead. She was some years older than he was and, although she was engaged and 'not to have', he fell desperately in love with her. She was flirtatious and took pleasure in the idolatry of the puffy schoolboy. Sick with unattainable love he refused to go back to school in September. He hung around her house and started to get on her nerves. His irritating idyll came to an abrupt end when he heard Mary say to her maid: 'What! Me care for that lame boy!' Shocked and enraged, he left the house. His infatuation may have cooled, but she remained his prototype of the ideal woman for the rest of his life.

His deformed foot always made him rebellious. In a letter to his pious literary friend Francis Hodgson, on 13 September 1811, in which he has a few strong words to say about Christianity, he also displays a humorous self-pity: 'And our carcases, which are to rise again, are they worth raising? I hope, if mine is, that I shall have a better pair of legs than I have moved on these two-and-twenty years, or I shall be sadly behind in the squeeze into Paradise.'

The deformity was an assault on his vanity, and on his temperament, as it prevented him from engaging in all kinds of activities.

Although, in a literary and cultural historical sense, the foot has become with hindsight *le défaut de sa qualité*, he himself never accepted it. At best, he compensated. Arnold's motto in *The Deformed Transformed* is: 'I love, and I shall be beloved'. Gabriël Matzneff suggests that Byron's turbulent love life was a continuous compensation for him feeling unloved because of his foot – as a child by his mother and later no less by himself.

Sport was another form of escape: fencing, boxing, shooting, but above all his passion for swimming and horse-riding. As a boy in Scotland, he had learned to swim in the Dee and the Don – in the water, he had no problems with his handicap. He became an inexhaustible swimmer who astounded friend and foe with his lack of fear and his stamina. In Portugal, he swam across the Tagus, at a point near the estuary notorious for its eddies and currents. In Turkey, together with an English lieutenant, he swam across the Hellespont, emulating the mythical Leander who secretly visited his lover every night in her tower on the seashore. It was to cost Leander his life on a stormy night. Hobhouse noted the event enthusiastically in his journal: today he had seen the myth with his own eyes! Byron himself, although proud of his achievement, wrote drily: 'The total distance E. and myself swam was more than 4 miles the current very strong and cold ... we were not fatigued but a little chilled; did it with little difficulty.' Six days later he recorded the event in the light-hearted verse 'Written after Swimming from Sestos to Abydos'. Many swimmers have since dared to make the crossing which, thanks to Byron, has acquired a romantic-heroic tint.

Years later, when Shelley was drowned during a sailing trip and Byron had to identify his washed-up body, he swam in the sea for four hours, devastated by the incident and by the fact that Shelley's handkerchief was unspoiled while the drowned body was recognisable only by the teeth. As a result, he contracted a bad cold and his shoulders were so sunburned that, a week later, Teresa Guiccioli was able to peel the skin off.

Lord Byron is long gone, but the peelings of his skin are not. One day, I went to find them. Although I found the idea ridiculous, I still wanted to see them.

One autumnal Monday morning I visited the Biblioteca Classensa in Ravenna, an ancient library housed in a former Capuchin monastery. When I said that I wanted to see the peelings of Byron's skin, the lady in charge of the archives appeared, armed with a large bunch of keys that looked as though they came from Blue-beard's castle. With clicking heels, she led through long halls with bookshelves two storeys high. There was no one there. As in all old libraries, the books seemed to be only of secondary importance; the building itself was a work of art, with balustrades of finely carved wood and ceilings painted in Baroque-style. We climbed up a floor and I was finally admitted to the Holy of Holies, announced by a bust of Byron's mistress Teresa Guiccioli.

This was the domain of a gaunt little man with white gloves, almost a shadow, whose only task seemed to be to guard the skin. With much rattling of the keys, he opened a safe. There was a solemn silence. The wait was tantalising – I momentarily expected the Great Swimmer himself to step out from behind a curtain. 'What kind of ridiculous display is this?' he would have said. 'The only good thing about life is its end, have peace with that.' Cardboard boxes were laid on the table and, with endless reverence, opened by the white-gloves. Now I had to control myself. With polite interest, feigning scientific objectivity, I examined the paraphernalia. From a rusty box emerged a small book from the 18th century, bound in purple velvet, the first chapter of which was about Vesuvius and the countryside around Naples. Inside the back cover, Byron had scribbled a letter to Teresa, dated 29 August 1819. I was permitted to hold the book and leaf through it.

Byron apologised for writing in English: '[...] but you will recog-nize the handwriting of him who passionately loved you [...].'

It was a strange, indescribable revelation to see and touch his original handwriting. My companion sat close to me like a chaper-one, watching everything I did. Then a box was placed in front of me filled to the brim with Byron's correspondence with Teresa. The letters were written on both sides of the paper, making the text – written in Italian in his elegant handwriting – difficult to read. There was no time to decipher them all, but in passing I did see that one of the letters ended boyishly with: 'I give you 10,000,000 kisses.' I counted the noughts.

Still no skin, but this time a collection of objects, each with a handwritten explanation by Teresa. When she was a middle-aged lady, she had ordered, catalogued and romanticised everything that reminded her of her famous lover. On one of the notes, for example, she had written: 'Wallpaper from the room where I usually received Lord Byron in my parents' house in Ravenna.' Wrapped in tissue paper were small strips of wallpaper, with broad stripes in ecru and cherry red, and a thin black stripe between them. They were made of silk and the colours were still very vivid. This small piece of wallpaper had seen more than I ever have. There was a ecru handkerchief, plissé, also wrapped in tissue paper, and with a note from Teresa: 'This was Lord Byron's handkerchief, and I kept it constantly with me during the illness that afflicted me as a result of the sorrow I suffered after Lord Byron left Venice.'

Then a portrait of Byron and Teresa in a flat, dark-red box. Her face had been erased. The librarian found her voice when she saw my amazement. 'It was a matter of ambiguity,' she said. 'Perhaps she did that at a time when her husband was jealous, so as not to be recognised together with Byron, but wanted very much to keep his portrait.' There was a caricature of the young Byron, portraying him as a piglet, and an enamel medallion of the poet in Venice. And, of course, locks of hair: a reddish-brown one of Teresa's and three dark brown ones from Bryon, cut off three years before his death and kept.

And finally, finally, the box with the pieces of skin was placed before me. Small, parchment-coloured slivers that may have contained sufficient genetic material to one day produce a clone. I would bet that if he were re-born Byron, with his love of the epic, would write novels rather than poems. In any case, a wondrous orthopaedic solution would be found for his foot, and Byron would no longer be Byron.

After his death Teresa undertook a pilgrimage to Newstead Abbey, as can be witnessed by the box containing beech nuts and dried rose petals from the estate. All these mementos of something that might not be forgotten, but which was certainly long dead, were a little morbid. It was a depressing thought that all that remained of passionate nights of love was a piece of wallpaper. All the items had been 'prepared by Savory, Moore and Davidson, Chemists to the Royal Family'. The last thing I leafed through was a thick manuscript, written in French by Teresa on Byron's life in Italy. Until now, no one had thought of publishing it. 'The book is on microfilm,' the guardian of the treasure told me. 'Someone asked about it recently. Perhaps there is some interest in it after all.'

Very much aware of my own mortality, I left the museum. No one will keep pieces of skin or locks of hair when I go; these are down-to-earth times.

Swimming was Byron's greatest joy. 'Water means freedom,' says

Matzneff philosophically. 'Water purifies and impregnates; it makes us unreachable.' As the years passed, Byron made sure he stayed fit. When he lived in Athens, he swam in the Saronic Gulf off Piraeus and later, while in Venice, in the Adriatic Sea and the Grand Canal. Countess Albrizzi delighted in recounting that Byron was once seen, 'on leaving a palace situated on the Grand Canal, instead of entering his own gondola, to throw himself into the water dressed as he was and swim to his lodging. To avoid the oars of the gondoliers, he carried a torch in his left hand when he swam in the canal at night.'

Horse-riding, his other passion, he had also learned at a young age. When he was riding, he – and others – could forget his foot. He organised his life so that he could ride every day, as his Italian journal reveals. On 15 January 1821, he wrote: 'Weather fine. Received visit. Rode out into the forest – fired pistols.' A day later: 'Read – rode – fired pistols – returned – dined – wrote – visited – heard music – talked nonsense – and went home.' On 17 January: 'Rode in the forest. Fired pistols. Went home.' If he missed a day, he felt that also worth mentioning: 'To-day, the post arriving late, did not ride.'

He continued to ride daily until 14 days before his death at Missolonghi on 19 April 1824. By then, his health had already deteriorated. He insisted on going riding, as heavy rainfall had made it impossible for several days. Pietro Gamba, Teresa's younger brother, who had accompanied him to Greece, reported later: 'Three miles from town, we were overtaken by a heavy rain, and we returned to the town walls wet through and in a violent perspiration.' Usually they returned by boat, but Gamba had insisted they go by horse otherwise Byron would have to sit still for half an hour, sweating and exposed to the elements. Although Byron was insulted – 'I should make a pretty soldier, indeed, if I were to care for such a trifle.' – he acquiesced with Gamba's proposal. 'Two hours after his return home,' wrote Gamba, who was as devoted a chronicler as his sister, 'he was seized with a shuddering. He complained of fever and rheumatic pains. At eight in the evening, I entered his room; he was lying on a sofa, restless and melancholy. He said to me: "I suffer a great deal of pain; I do not care for death; but these agonies I cannot bear".'

Nevertheless he was back on his horse the following day, with pains in his bones and a headache. In good spirits, he rode for a long time through the olive trees with Pietro and his bodyguard. When he returned, he scolded his groom for allowing him to ride on the wet saddle from the previous day. It was his last ride. His illness increased in severity and Byron worried about a prediction that had been made to him when he was a boy in Scotland: 'Beware your 37th year.' When he was accused of being superstitious, he defended himself by saying: 'To say the truth, I find it equally difficult to know what to believe in this world, and what not to believe...'

Was riding his horse in bad weather fatal for Byron? There are many theories about the cause of his death, including marsh fever, malaria and exhaustion. The most popular is that his doctors killed him with an excess of goodwill and bloodletting. The latter had allegedly increased the uric acid content in his blood to such a level that he died of severe poisoning.

Opinions vary as to whether he could ride as well as he swam. Medwin called him an 'excellent rider', while Lady Blessington, who he met in Genoa not long before his death, claimed that he was mediocre and a little timid.

One thing is certain: when he travelled through Albania on horseback, he was young, healthy and buoyant: 'I rode out on the viziers horses,' he boasted to his mother. He must have felt himself a hero from one of Sir Water Scott's tales of gallant knights, and an intrepid explorer in the Oriental world he had dreamed of as a child: 'Albania indeed I have seen more of than any Englishman [...].' New horizons, adventures, exoticism, freedom, loose morals, young company..., anything was fine as long as it pushed the memory of England into the background.

His letters exude youthful exuberance: 'I smoke, and stare at mountains, and twirl my mustachios very independently. I miss no comforts [...].' Veli Pasha, Ali's son who he met later, recommended that his 'Albanians' heads should be cut off if they behaved ill'.

Byron himself lost neither his head nor his innocence. The latter he had lost long before.

# Chapter 14

MY DEAR FRIEND, I was awakened by an insistent American voice. American? There was no doubt about it, but it was mixed in with staccato primal sounds. Daniël's bed was empty. I threw my clothes on and hurried off in the direction of the racket. With one eye I saw Daniël and our host fraternally sitting and watching an American television programme, with the other I could see an old radio from which polyphonic shepherds' voices could be heard. Perhaps the teacher saw silent reproach in my expression as I poked my head around the corner, as he stood up quickly and switched the radio off.

I went outside. My towel was hanging ready in the open-air bathroom. The teacher's wife pointed to my trousers, which I had washed the night before. She took them off the line and went inside to hang them over an electric radiator. Her thoughtfulness was moving. Smiling silently, she stayed close to me to make sure that I had every comfort. When I admired the blossom on an orange tree, she plucked the whole branch for me. When I was careless enough to point to a tree full of mandarins, she gave me as many as I could carry. After that I no longer dared to show my appreciation for anything; she would have given me everything she owned. Anxiously I recalled the strict rules of traditional Albanian hospitality.

We ate a breakfast of thick yogurt and home-made plum jam, while on the television we were urged to buy a machine you could use to stretch your body. Women in tight fitness clothing demonstrated with smiles from ear to ear the exceptional benefits of this instrument of torture. We were then abruptly transported to an American kitchen, where someone used a trumped up grater to dice and slice vegetables with, as the *pièce de résistance*, a carrot cut into a spiral. At eight o'clock in the morning, the teacher could see how superfluous demand is created from nothing in our profligate consumer society.

Our departure was again accompanied by expansive expressions of gratitude. I wanted to take a picture of the couple on the veranda – sending them a photo was the least I could do after they had made us so welcome. The wife disappeared inside for a long time to make herself presentable but, when she did finally emerge, it was a complete metamorphosis: she was wearing a black suit with white buttons and high heels. 'Very elegant!' I exclaimed, and she smiled with disbelief. They posed shyly, and then we all walked in a procession down the bumpy path, the wife tottering along on her high heels, grasping her black handbag tightly. The couple had decided to ride with our driver to Gjirokastër and make a day of it.

The new horseman was waiting for us with an engaging smile. Next to him was a dour, suntanned boy in a coarse woollen jumper that he never took off, even when it became very hot. The father of this 'dragoboy', who I guessed was around 14, was the owner of the second horse. It was a clear day, and everything was full-coloured and shining in the sun. Watched as usual by an audience of men and children, I clambered up onto one of the horses, a grey, while Daniël mounted the other one, a glossy roan. And off we went again, this time much more relaxed. Clearly, it didn't always have to be such a struggle.

The landscape was now open on all sides, with robust mountains in the distance. We no longer followed the flank of the mountain. Hobhouse's account of the geography of this part of the journey was once again open to many interpretations: 'On leaving Ereeneed, on the morning of the 19th, at ten o'clock, we descended from the hills, and got into the plain, through which, in a north-westerly direction, ran the river we had crossed in going from Libokavo to Cesarades.' He makes it sound as though they were down on the plain in a trice. He conveniently forgets to mention the plateau that you have to cross first.

In the middle of the plateau, which was completely devoid of signs of human habitation, there was a small, one-room Orthodox chapel dedicated to St. George. Judging from the roof, which had half collapsed, it had long ago been abandoned to the elements. And yet someone had taken the trouble to place an icon of the Saint and a Madonna with Child in the protection of a recess, and to light a candle. A shepherd, perhaps. We had seen plenty of them on our way, with flocks of sheep or goats. Yogurt and cheese must have been the salvation of the Albanians.

Under the watchful eye of St George, Daniël dismounted from his horse to make way for the Professor, who climbed up with gruff impatience. Just as you thought he was going to slide off the other side, he managed to stay in the saddle. It would never be his favourite mode of transport. I was also starting to feel the first signs of discomfort: the insides of my knees and thighs were chafing. Daniël, who always rode side-saddle – which I quietly thought a little frumpy – advised me to do the same. I tried it and he was right, it was as though you were sitting in an armchair. Unconsciously I had cherished a heroic image of Mongols galloping over the steppes, while here in the mountains of Albania, everyone we met was riding side-saddle.

When we came to a flat meadow, Roberto suggested that we try some shooting practice – not suspecting that he was acting entirely in your spirit. He placed a cola can on a tree stump a respectable distance away in the field and drew his gun from his belt. He aimed, shot and missed. We were smitten by an attack of hilarity. Karagjozi and Daniël also wanted to know how a pistol felt in their hands. Giggling nervously, they allowed Roberto to show them how to use it. Since the armed attack promised by *Le Monde* had not materialised, we had to make our own excitement. Afrim adopted a martial stance, all humour gone. Suddenly, it was serious. He held the barrel at eye level and concentrated. The cola can was still standing there on the scaffold, challenging him. Seeing the Professor with a weapon was even more ludicrous than seeing him on a horse. Not every Albanian had the genes of a bandit. He fired, and the bullet disappeared into the nothingness without hitting the can. Daniël suffered the same fate.

My own aspirations were aroused. Just imagine if I, as the only woman, could hit the target. I recalled your own boasting about your accuracy: 'Good shooting – broke four common, and rather small, bottles, in four shots, at fourteen paces, with a common pair of pistols and indifferent powder.' I tapped Roberto on the shoulder. As if it were the most normal thing in the world, he laid the pistol in my hand – it was wonderfully cool and smooth. He showed me how to hold it at arm's length and pull the trigger. Scenes from films and television series raced through my head. 'Holy Mary, Calamity Jane...' I muttered and fired. Less than a second later, I was dancing around like a dervish with my fingers in my ears, startled by the enormous bang and the power it released. Everyone was enjoying my discomfort. The cola can was still standing upright, undamaged. Now we all clamoured to have another shot, but Roberto had no more bullets. I would have liked to try it again, and again. A single shot was enough to help me understand a little better this favourite pastime of yours, which until then I had considered a little dubious.

We continued on our way. I couldn't find a suitable rock to help me climb back onto the horse. Roberto showed me how to jump up into the side-saddle position in one leap. Feeling reckless after the shooting practice, I gave it a try. And there I was, in the saddle. Roberto was clearly impressed. 'You mount a horse like a true Shqiptar,' he laughed.

I myself thought I was starting to look more and more like an 'Albanian virgin'. In the traditional clan society in the remote regions of Albanian, women were always considered inferior beings. There was a saying that 'a woman should work harder than a donkey, because a woman eats bread and a donkey eats grass'. As soon as they were sexually mature, women were married off, veiled, and transported to their husband's house. There they would spend the rest of their lives, as the property of their family-in-law, mostly far away from their place of birth. The dowry included a bullet, as the husband was entitled to kill his wife if she were unfaithful to him. The life of a married woman consisted of working and bearing children, preferably sons. In a patriarchal society, where everything passed through the male line, the family with only daughters was worth nothing. For a woman who wanted to escape this fate, there was only one option: to become a man. The woman would have to make a public pledge never to marry and to remain a virgin, dress as a man, carry weapons and, if necessary, fight as a soldier. If there were no other men in the family, she could even become the head of the family and make all the important decisions. The English artist Edith Durham, who travelled through the most inaccessible mountainous areas of Albania at the start of the 20th century, described in her book *High Albania* a woman who had made this choice: 'Here [in the village of Rapsha] we found one of the Albanian virgins who wear male attire. While we halted to water the horses she came up – a lean, wiry, active woman of forty-seven, clad in very ragged garments, breeches and coat. She was highly amused at being photographed, and the men chaffed her about her "beauty." She had dressed as a boy, she said, ever since she was quite a child because she had wanted to, and her father had let her. Of matrimony she was very derisive–all her sisters were married, but she had known better.'

The sun burned down on our heads. I was jealous of Afrim Karagjozi's baseball cap. Even better, I would have liked a white headscarf like those worn by the women who worked on the land, ingeniously folded into a peak. We moved through the landscape at the languid pace of four hooves, a good lesson or remedy for those of us who are so accustomed to making haste. Before me, I saw the trade caravans that used to trek along the Via Egnatia from the Albanian coast to Constantinople, or through these southern mountains to Ioannina and Athens. How long did it take them? What a difference to our heavy trucks, whose drivers – paid by commission – race along the motorways to deliver fresh vegetables or cut flowers from the auction to Rome or Madrid in the space of a single day. What did the merchants of old think about during those long journeys? They had plenty of time and silence in which to ponder as they moved with a sluggish rhythm through the continually changing landscape. Time and silence have become scarce goods in the Western Europe of the 20th century. We live on top of each other in cities that are bursting at the seams, and have become so afraid of time that all we can do is kill it.

During the journey from Erind to Tepelene, Hobhouse had fantasised about the Greek and Roman armies which reportedly used the gorges carved out by rivers to march eastwards through almost impenetrable mountains and conquer Macedonia. It was possible, because Pyrrhus had done it previously – with elephants – in 288 BC, to breathe new life into the former empire of Alexander the Great.

We entered a village with the bizarre name of Hundëkuq. One front garden was filled by a tractor, lovingly covered in cloths. At a strategic point, a cafe had just been built. At the entrance another pair of police officers stood waiting for us. Were they not exaggerating a little? After all, we had Roberto with us. But they had only come to make sure that we had not disappeared somewhere in the immeasurable wilderness. And, of course, we had to drink to the encounter. Inside, it smelled of fresh wood and paint. Cigarettes and Dutch beer were placed on the table. Men we did not know joined us. The purpose of our journey again invoked widespread surprise. You could see them wavering between mockery and respect, and as more and more beer was consumed, the former gained the upper hand.

But we had to move on, to complete the final stretch on horseback.

The Drino came into sight, a silver ribbon in the landscape. On its banks, the white gravel glistened between the lush green of plane trees, poplars and willows. Because the path continued in the wrong direction we crossed a turnip field. The horses ploughed their way through black clumps of earth, while birds that were pecking at seeds flew up in to the air in fright. On the other side of the field, a spindly woman with a black hood on her head was tending to her turkeys, bunches of feathers that she kept together with a stick. Then, in the distance, between the trees, we saw the bridge.

Hobhouse records a notable encounter when you arrived at this place: 'After travelling down the valley an hour we came in sight of a bridge, and saw crossing it a large Party of soldiers, and some Turks on horseback, attending a covered chair or litter. A little after, to our great surprise, we were met by a carriage, not ill-made, but in the German fashion, with a man on the box driving four-in-hand, and two dirty Albanian soldiers standing on the foot-board behind. They were floundering on at a trot through the mire; but how it would be possible for them to pass over part of the road by which we had come, we did not at all understand. However, the population of whole villages was ordered out to help it along, and we heard afterwards of its safe arrival at Libokavo. This carriage had, as they told us, conveyed a lady of the Vizier's harem to the bridge, where she was met by the chair (a large sedan), in which she was to be carried on men's shoulders to Tepellenè.'

This is a very appealing *tableau vivant*. But there are no more coaches, no harem ladies, no Viziers, and of the arched stone bridge, only two pillars and a few of the arches above the river banks were still intact. A less than idyllic rusty Bailey bridge now joined the two banks. As we approached the bridge, I felt very close to you. Here, our footsteps literally came together. You had to dismount because the arch of the bridge was too steep for the horses; we had to dismount because it was the end of our journey on horseback. Motorised horsepower would take us on from here. The horses were put out to graze in a field next to the old bridge, and we all crossed the bridge – one foot at a time, as there were planks missing, while others were broken or splintered.

On the other side, there was a cafe. A flat box with no trace of ornamentation or imagination. At this important junction there must have once been an old 'han'. Some places are made for introspection and prayer, and have churches or chapels built on them.

Others have always been natural watering holes, where travellers stop to drink or smoke a pipe. There you will find a bar. We greeted our driver and Hadji, who had come along with him, and sat down at an outside table. This was the moment for a final toast. We were sitting in a large circle, which was about to be broken. The horse-man and his assistant would return to Erind that same day, without even taking so much as a lunchbox of bread with them. We complimented the horse-man and thanked him for making the journey so pleasurable – it was good to know that it didn't have to end in disaster. He was content – he had completed his unusual mission.

We drank to each other's health and said our farewells. Shoulder slaps, photos and then we climbed into the bus with the curtains to head for Tepelene.

'Immediately after getting across we went along a path on the ledge of a steep precipice, with the river, which was broad (perhaps seventy feet), deep, and very rapid, rolling underneath.'

The ledge along which you had to carefully pick your way is now an asphalt road. After the silence of the mountains, the drone of the engines was an assault on the soul, somehow devastatingly aggressive. How could we live with that? And at what expense? On the road, there were a lot of Mercedes cars, trucks from Western countries, and Russian or Chinese-made buses. The cars often had broken windscreens or no licence plates. Anything goes in Albania – they were still a long way from compulsory tests of roadworthiness. Daniël wondered out loud where all the cars had suddenly come from. He had been in Tirana four years previously and no one had a car at all then. Alongside the road, there were tomb-like shrines commemorating the victims of fatal accidents. There were also much older memorials for dead partisans, from which everything of value – marble or bronze – had been stripped. Was there no longer any respect for the heroes of the past? Seven kilometres from Tepelene we passed a famous cold-water spa, where in Hoxha's time, a kind of tea-garden had been built to help the workers and their comrades relax.

We were now travelling at such a speed that I lost sight of you. We rushed ahead, leaving the 19th century and its still human pace behind – and yet I had the feeling that I could not catch up with you. Hobhouse's journal describes your slow approach to the city, how it extended your sense of expectation and curiosity: 'In two hours from the bridge the river began to widen considerably, and a little way farther it was augmented by a stream of some breadth, flowing out of a narrow valley from the north-east. Not long after the junction of the rivers, the whole stream appeared as broad as the Thames at Westminster-bridge, but looking shallow in many places, with gravel banks above the water. Soon afterwards we had a view of Tepellenè, the termination of our journey, which we saw situated immediately on the bank of the river, and in three-quarters of an hour we entered the native place of Ali.'

Tepelene. The bus bumped into the city over crumbling asphalt. From behind the curtains, I saw flaky plaster, decaying concrete, broken and boarded-up windows, bare paintwork and refuse. Hoxha should have lived to see the long-term consequences of his policy of having flats built by neighbours and by intellectuals who had to do forced manual labour for one month a year. He felt that professional builders should focus on 'more important projects', like factories, cultural centres and cinemas.

The streets of Tepelene were lined with the stumps of what had once been trees.

'Chopped down for fuel in the winter of '91, when the people were starving,' said Karagjozi laconically. The pavements were in a bad state of repair, everything was muddy, and wrecked cars and piles of rubbish were strewn around.

Against this backdrop, the streets were full of hustle and bustle. Again, I saw the stalls consisting of a piece of cloth with two sticks, cardboard boxes or orange crates – somewhere in passing I saw one selling nothing but hubcaps. The inhabitants hung around, some apathetically, others with pent-up energy, or even tensed up. In a park, at the foot of three busts of heroes from the Second World War, a group of men were sitting on a neglected lawn playing cards. I was struck by how many children there were. 'Two of every three Albanians are under the age of 30,' I had read in my travel guide. Perhaps an attempt to compensate for all the Albanians who had left the country through the centuries, to go to Greece and Italy, or even cross the oceans to the United States and Australia.

We stopped at the town hall. Karagjozi told us there was a woman there who knew we were coming. Because the only hotel in Tepelene was, according to Daniël's travel guide, the worst in the whole of Albania, Afrim had written to the mayor and, through him, had arranged accommodation in a former hotel for top Party officials. It was higher up the mountain, on the edge of the city. The mayor, who was not available that day, was to be represented by the woman. Karagjozi disappeared into the town hall. After a long wait, he was told that the woman was not there, but in Gjirokastër. It looked as though we would have to find our way into the holiday sanctum ourselves.

The bus bumped uphill until the high-rise buildings stopped and we entered a more prosperous district. Here many of the Communist-style houses, less close together and surrounded by gardens, could easily have been candidates for a Party hotel. While we waited, sitting on a stone wall in the shadow of cypress trees, the professor went to take a look. As I sat staring at the shabby city spread out below, I tried to repress the feeling of dejection that was slowly taking hold of me. I re-read Hobhouse's description of your arrival: 'The streets of the town, through which we passed, were dirty and ill-built.' That was some comfort: in your time, too, Tepelene was a dismal sight to behold. That only increased your surprise when you entered the domain of Ali Pasha: '... but everything that had before attracted our attention was presently forgotten, when we entered through a gateway in a tower, and found ourselves in the court-yard of the Vizier's palace.'

So, where was the palace? You trotted straight into a thousand-and-one-nights fairy-tale, but we were sitting on a wall wondering where we were going to sleep. A blonde man of about 25 came strolling past, so bright and shining in comparison with the Albanians we had seen that he could only be a North American – one of those you see in commercials surfing off the coast of California.

'Hi.' He raised a hand, cheerily. Apparently, he could see immediately that we were not Shqiptars. He stopped to have a chat – he seemed to have all the time in the world. He was not at all surprised to hear about our mission – though I must admit that, in comparison, his was a lot more absurd. He was a member of a Protestant church from Vancouver and had come to Tepelene to save souls and do social work.

'Which church?' I asked.

'No special denomination,' he answered vaguely. 'We adapt ourselves to the situation. It has to be a real Albanian variant, you know...' His girlfriend was here too, and other members of the church were active in Tepelene and the surrounding area. After a lot of red tape, they now had their own building and were doing it up.

Later Karagjozi told me that, in the vacuum left after the fall of Communism, religious groups from the East and West were trying to get a foothold in Albania before the competition did so. The Muslims were the most successful, and new mosques were being built all over the country. It was only rarely that you would see a new Roman Catholic or Greek Orthodox church.

Albania was an early Christian country. After the schism in Christianity, the north became Catholic and the south Orthodox. Under the Turkish occupation, the country gradually became more and more Islamised, not by force, but in a much more ingenious fashion. You had to have very strong religious convictions to resist the temptation of a plot of land or a substantial tax cut – incentives used to persuade people to pray with their head bowed towards Mecca. Most of us sell our souls to the devil for less. If the Catholics had applied this method at the time instead of the Inquisition, they would definitely have been much more successful. The majority of Albanians therefore converted to the Sunni faith of the occupiers, though the Bektashi movement became popular with a small minority.

This tolerant, mystical variant of Islam, which also contains pagan and Christian elements, was established in the 16th century by the dervish Hajji Bektash Wali from the province of Khorasan in Persia. His followers (who still exist, especially in Anatolia) believe in the Holy Trinity and the Twelve Apostles; they also recognise confession as a means of forgiveness. In addition to the men, the women – unveiled – also take part in festive rituals. They drink wine or raki and dance together to religious music. Everything is very civilised and nothing at all untoward happens, despite rumours of orgies circulating among more orthodox Muslims, resulting in the persecution and killing of many Bektashis. The movement seems to practice a kind of ecumenism *avant la lettre*, as they accept believers from other faiths in their midst without them having to give up their original religion. They must have had a strong appeal, as Ali Pasha himself secretly joined their ranks around 1800.

Before the Communists banned the Church and religion, 70% of Albanians were Muslims, 20% Greek Orthodox and 10% Roman Catholic. The Greek Orthodox believers lived mainly in the south, in and around the cities of Gjirokastër and Korça. In the Ottoman Empire, the Albanians were never considered a separate people. For the occupiers, the Muslims were Turks, the Orthodox Christians were Greeks and the Catholics Italians. A person's nationality was thus determined by their religion. It is not clear whether this was a clever example of divide and rule but, in any case, it certainly limited the development of a sense of national unity for many centuries.

Hoxha did not deal with the Church all at once, but in stages. Initially religious gatherings were not banned, just thwarted. From 1967, following the example of the Chinese Revolution, he initiated a number of anti-religious campaigns to 'embed in the people the ideology of scientific materialism'. Young people were allocated an active role in these campaigns. Churches and mosques were either demolished or given a secular purpose as sports centres, museums or cultural centres, symbolised by a red star on their spires or minarets. Imams and priests were re-educated to become normal citizens. The Catholic church in Shkodra, once the Vatican of Albania, became an atheist museum with a permanent exhibition of photographs and documents depicting the success of the campaign. As the early Christians preferred to build their churches on the holy sites of the pagans, the young atheists returned them to their original heathen state. *Panta rhei* – all things flow, and sometimes they all flow back again.

It was even forbidden to give new-born babies Christian names. Anyone who wanted to climb the Party ladder was well advised to give their children Illyrian names.

Whether all these measures actually succeeded in eradicating religion from the lives of the Albanians will become clear in the coming years. Will all the newly built houses of God, still smelling of fresh cement, fill up with believers? When I asked what he thought, the Professor pulled an ugly face. Close to his house in Tirana a muezzin has recently again started calling the faithful to prayer – all nonsense in his opinion, not to mention noisy. 'If the Albanians feel the need to start believing again, why don't they become Catholics? After all, we were traditionally Christians, not Muslims.'

We took our leave of the cheerful missionary. 'Good luck!' He gave a carefree laugh and strode off resolutely. For him, everything was easy and certain. I envied him. Where did he get such self-confidence and certainty, in a desperate country like Albania? The only answer could be that he was filled with the glory of God. I wondered how many unsuspecting Albanians he would lure into his temple-clubhouse in the guise of providing social assistance.

In the meantime, Karagjozi had found the hotel, and a man who guarded the grounds. After the Professor had told him the whole story, together they forced the lock. The hotel was a perfect example of Communist megalomania. Everything was disproportionately large – the hall, the stairway, the bedrooms and the beds, the bath-room and the dining room, with covers over the chairs and a gigantic wall unit in which the two-headed eagle was carved in wood. The browns and beiges of the 1950s and 1960s dominated, and everything was in dire need of restoration. The bad taste and severity were as revolting as the prevalence of imitation was ridiculous.

The Professor, with his incurable gallantry, allocated me the room in which the district head of the Party slept whenever he visited Tepelene. One look at this elite suite was enough to make me shrink back with revulsion. I knew that I would not get a wink of sleep in this immense, upholstered coffin full of black leather arm-chairs. A repressive gloominess hung over the room that was prob-ably intended to be dignified. Instead I hastily chose a slightly more cheerful room for Party bigwigs, with a three-person bed and a view over the dilapidated flats of Tepelene – but at least I could see the mountains beyond them.

I washed a few shirts and socks and hung them here and there to dry. With the washing draped over the arms of chairs and radiator knobs, the room immediately looked a little more human. Then I collapsed onto the massive bed and lay there for a while, my arms and legs spread out. A sense of deep alienation washed over me. Why was I here and not somewhere else? There was nothing to suggest that I was close to Ali Pasha's serail. I was here in this ersatz building. Outside it was already dusk and I would have to suppress my impatience until tomorrow. You could never in your wildest dreams imagine the situation I now found myself in, in the Albania of today. You died before Karl Marx had written *Das Kapital*, a book that would change the world much more dramatically than your *Childe Harold*. How could I explain that to you? I sniffed dis-tractedly at a bunch of mountain tea. Ah, the smell of the country we had travelled through.

They were all sitting together in the hall. We chatted about the trip and paid the driver. I quietly slipped a token of my gratitude into the hands of Roberto and Hadji. Until now they had firmly refused any form of remuneration for their help, but now they were secretly pleased to accept it. It was as though we had known each other for years, and we parted as old friends. A 'Mirupafshim!' that would never be realised, and our dragomen disappeared, leaving us behind with the guard, who crept gloomily and silently through the building.

It was time for dinner. Afrim Karagjozi brought along a large torch, anticipating the absence of streetlights. We walked downhill between the flats. Although there were still many people on the streets, the atmosphere was still sinister, for some inexplicable reason. Four men raced past in a Mercedes, visible through the windows as thick heads of hair above leather jackets with large zips. 'Maffiosi,' said the Professor, sombre. 'In Tirana, they are called "the Powerful".'

It took me a while to realise that we were standing in front of the walls of Ali Pasha's citadel, which were built of large blocks of stone, mostly grey, some blackened. 'I'm sure there was a restaurant around here somewhere,' Karagjozi mumbled, looking around with a frown. Hope flared up. Would we make those first magical steps through the gateway and into another world today, after all? The Professor found the restaurant, but was told that they only served meat – no potatoes, no vegetables, nothing. He shook his head. What was this country coming to, if you couldn't get vegetables in a restaurant? You could say what you liked about Hoxha, but in his time, vegetable production was so high, there was enough over to export. With hunger gnawing at our stomachs we walked further alongside the wall.

In passing the Professor shone his torch on a bronze plaque with your likeness. You were wearing your Albanian turban and there was an olive branch next to your left arm. The old plaque had been destroyed, Karagjozi told us, and he had made every effort to ensure that it was replaced with a new one. A friend had cast it and he himself had written the text, placed together with a quotation from *Childe Harold*. I believe – credit where credit is due – the Professor is the only person in the whole of Albania who makes sure your name is not forgotten.

We carried on searching for a restaurant, but found nothing, not even the simplest eating house. There were trucks parked everywhere – Tepelene was clearly the last stop before the Greek border. So where did all the drivers eat? Alienated and with a growing sense of unease, we wandered through the dark centre of the city.

Through the open door of a cafe I saw on old man with a beard and a hat, sitting at a bare table. He was leaning forward and dozing. His crutch, which he must have needed to walk, had slipped down with him and was blocking the way. Someone will fall over that, I said to myself, and break a leg and need a crutch to walk, which some-body else will fall over, and so on. I suddenly thought that is what has happened to Albania for centuries, the same misery recurring over and again, *mise en abyme*, with no one to blame. On the table in front of the man, who was wearing a T-shirt with the text 'American Tennis Good', lay an open notebook and a pencil. His right hand was resting on the paper. What had he wanted to write? Had it asked so much of his weary brain that he had drifted off into sleep? Was he Homer reincarnated, who had resolved this time to write the history of the Balkans? Then he had better wake up quickly, and stay awake. I thought all this in a flash, and it put me in a even more sombre mood. Somehow, the sleeping man seemed to reveal more than everything I had seen and heard so far.

A group of people passed for whom even the term *nouveau riche* was a euphemism. Men wearing brightly coloured jogging suits with thick, gold-coloured wristwatches, rings and chains – in the company of women dolled up in the same way. Why did they seem to adopt mostly the ugly aspects of the West? Like caricatures, they struck a contrast with the other people in the street, in their worn suit-jackets over flocky, washed-out jumpers.

We had nearly given up when, at the edge of the city centre, we came across a brand-new restaurant. A woman with a robust body and a stern jaw spoke to us with the charm of a hippopotamus. Yes, she admitted with reluctance, they served potatoes and salad with the meat. We rushed to sit down. The Professor relaxed and, with a wide gesture, ordered a large dish of roast leg of lamb.

When the meal arrived I attacked it in a most un-ladylike fashion. But we were clearly having a bad evening. A leg of lamb is a piece of dead animal – you have to be content with that knowledge – but this lamb was certainly very dead. I spat the rotten meat out as inconspicuously as possible and took a large mouthful of potatoes to take away the taste. But the Professor had noticed. 'Off,' I said softly, adding remorsefully: 'But it's alright, I'll just eat more potatoes.'

As I feared, he took it personally. Agitated, he stuck his fork into his own meat and tasted it. His was OK, did I want to swap? No, no, I replied evasively, it was actually better for my stomach not to eat meat anyway. Daniël came to my defence: his meat was not so much off as very raw. His face tense, the Professor continued to eat. I ordered an extra plate of potatoes.

The bill was absurdly high. Although Daniël and I insisted on paying, Karagjozi was seriously upset. 'I feel very bad,' he sighed, his head in his hands. We tried to console him, telling him it was alright, we were prepared for anything.

The torch proved to have been a good idea for finding our way back to the hotel. The guard was waiting for us, a lost figure standing with eyes cast down in the enormous hall, suggesting some great drama in his past or future.

'Why does he look so sad?' I whispered.

'Because he is slowly going blind. He is still young, only 36, but in the past few years his eyesight has been deteriorating at an alarming pace. He can no longer distinguish colours and his response to light and dark is diminishing. He was an officer in the army when he first contracted the disease, and he has a wife and two children.'

I asked if he could be operated on. 'In Albania?' The Professor replied with a dry laugh. No, his only chance of a cure lay in the hands of a group of Italian hunters – lawyers, doctors and teachers – who stayed in the hotel once a year to go hunting in the mountains. They had offered to pay for him to go to Italy for treatment. But a strange problem had arisen. The Italian Embassy was refusing to issue him with a visa. He had been trying for years, but to no avail. Perhaps, in the past, there had been a criminal with the same name, or his photo looked like someone who was not welcome in Italy. He could not find out what the problem was. As he wrestled with this mystery, day in, day out, his eyesight was getting steadily worse and the day that he would also have to give up this job was coming closer.

'But,' Afrim said, 'I know someone at the embassy. Perhaps I can do something for him.'

I took a step towards the guard to say something to cheer him up, but what could you say to someone whose future was in the hands of the Italian bureaucracy which, as everyone knows, functions – or dysfunctions, who was to say? – on the basis of error and misappropriation. Slowly I was starting to feel the powerlessness that held the people of this country in a stranglehold – without assistance from outside, Albania would never be able to pull itself up out of the gutter.

To rinse away the feeling of despondency, I took a bath in the enormous bathroom. The bath was grimy, like everything in the hotel, but a strong stream of warm water came out of the tap. Grasping the sides so as not to drown in the tub, which could have held three Party bigwigs at the same time, I thought of how times had changed. You and Hobhouse were received with full pomp and ceremony by a jumped-up bandit who decided arbitrarily on the fate of his subjects. Nine years later, Marx was born – and, as a result, I was lying here in a bath designed for Party bigwigs. Between then and now, the world had changed beyond recognition. For better or for worse? That was the question that I kept asking myself because my constant, perhaps unhealthy, desire for the past filled me with scepticism. The dubious longing for a time in which men were roasted alive and women were drowned in jute sacks, could only exist because of the enormous time difference between 1809 and 1996, which had even given Ali Pasha's cruelty a bronze glow like the ancient light that illuminated the landscape here every afternoon. It gave his cruelty a kind of beauty of its own, which became part of the exotic atmosphere that surrounded him and filled you with passion.

In my king-size bed, Albanian-style, I felt the whole time that I was laying between Dulla and Sorra. The ghosts of Albania's recent past hung in the room, frustrated at their loss of face.

The contrast between my accommodation and yours was stark: 'On our arrival we were informed that we were to be lodged in the palace; and, accordingly, dismounting, we ascended a flight of wooden steps into a long gallery with two wings, opening into which, as in a large English inn, were the doors of several apartments. Into one of these we were shown, and found ourselves lodged in a chamber fitted up with large silken sofas, and having another room above it for sleeping; a convenience scarcely ever to be met with in Turkey. His Highness (for so the Pashas of the three tails are called by their attendant Greeks) sent a congratulatory message to us on our arrival, ordering everything to be provided for us by his own household; and mentioning, at the same time, that he was sorry the Ramazan prevented him from having our company with him at one of his repasts. He ordered, however, that sherbets, sweetmeats, and fruits, should be sent to us from his own harem.'

# Chapter 15

'HE TOLD ME to consider him as a father whilst I was in Turkey, & said he looked on me as his son. Indeed he treated me like a child, sending me almonds & sugared sherbet, fruit & sweetmeats 20 times a day.'

Ali Pasha took extremely great care of Lord Byron. Why? Surely not only because he had 'had small ears, curling hair, & little white hands'? In what situation did Byron find himself when he entered the gate of the citadel?

The Pasha was an astute statesman. When he heard that a young Englishman, and a noble to boot, was passing through his lands, he must have stroked his white beard and wondered whether a visitor of such stature might not be of use to him in his efforts at foreign diplomacy. During the Napoleonic Wars, he had remained on friendly terms with England, France and Russia. The English Admiral Nelson, the Russian Tsar and Napoleon all saw the Pasha and his fight for independence as a potentially important instrument in their efforts to further weaken the ailing Ottoman Empire, which had become known as the 'Sick Man of Europe'.

'Napoleon has twice offered to make him King of Epirus,' Byron wrote to his mother. 'But he prefers the English interest & abhors the French as he himself told me, he is of so much consequence that he is courted by both, the Albanians being the most warlike subjects of the Sultan, though Ali is only nominally dependent on the Porte. [...] Bonaparte sent him a snuff box with his picture[;] he said the snuff box was very well, but the picture he could excuse, as he neither liked *it* nor the *original*.'

Hobhouse gives another example of Napoleon's gifts. One evening, during one of their audiences, Ali showed them some pistols and a sabre. He saved the best for last: a present from the French

Emperor. It was a rifle, with the stock inlaid in silver, studded with diamonds and brilliants. The friends were impressed, but later were told by the Secretary that 'when the gun came from Napoleon, it had only a common stock, and that all the ornaments had been added by his Highness, to make it look more like a Royal gift'.

Hobhouse, who always did his homework to the extreme, investigated his host's past thoroughly. He discovered that Ali had been born into a relatively simple family around 1750. His father was a Pasha of two territories, but of no great importance. 'Our attendant Vasilly [...] assured me, that he recollects, when a boy, to have seen Ali [...] in his father's cottage, with his jacket out at elbows; and that, at that time, this person used to come with parties from Tepellenè in the night, and seize upon the flocks of the villages at enmity with him.' Taking one village after another, Ali Pasha succeeded in amassing money and power. His henchmen, a group of professional robbers, were paid in plunder – at that time also a customary way of complementing soldiers' salaries. Eventually he had enough money to buy a *pashalik*, from which he could continue to wage war. He succeeded in conquering Ioannina, and was officially declared Pasha of three inheritable territories by the Sultan in Constantinople.

But Ali could think of nothing other than enlarging his possessions. 'He then made war on the Pashas of Arta, of Delvino, and of Orcida, whom he subdued, together with that of Triccola, and established a very preponderating influence over the Agas of Thessaly.'

He did not shirk from the cruellest of methods to achieve his aims. He had Giaffar, Pasha of Vallona, poisoned by a cup of coffee in a bath, and then married his two sons Mouctar and Veli to the daughters of Giaffar's brother Ibrahim. He continued to harass the latter, adding considerably to his territories around Ioannina. He then had to conquer *pashaliks* for Mouctar and Veli. But Veli had been saving up and was able to buy the *pashalik* of the Morea for 15,000 piasters, together with the dignity of Vizier. Mouctar, who was very militarisitic, took his father's place at the head of the Albanians who had been sent to fight in the armies of the Sultan and distinguished himself there.

According to Hobhouse, the main opposition Ali Pasha encountered in expanding his power did not come from the other Pashas, but from the much more difficult to control 'nature of the people, and of the country of which he was determined to make himself master. Many of the parts which now compose his dominions were peopled by inhabitants who had been always in rebellion, or had never been entirely conquered by the Turks; such as the Chimeriotes, the Suliotes, and other tribes living amongst the mountains in the neighbourhood of the Ionian Sea. Besides this, the woods and hills of every part of his government were, in a manner, in possession of large bands of robbers, who were recruited and housed in the villages, and who laid large tracts under contribution, burning and plundering the districts under the Pasha's protection. Against these he proceeded with the greatest severity: they were burnt, hanged, beheaded, and impaled, and have disappeared from many parts, especially of Upper Albania, which were before quite subject to these outlaws.'

Whether he liked it or not, Hobhouse was impressed by the rapid rise of this boy from the mountains to become the Pasha of a self-created empire and who had no intention as yet of resting on his laurels: '[...]and, should his projects of aggrandisement succeed, the countries which anciently composed the southern part of Illyricum, the kingdom of Epirus, part of Macedonia, the whole Thessalian territory, Euboea, and all the Grecian states, will be under the dominion of a barbarian who can neither write nor read.'

There were two diametrically opposed views on Ali Pasha, both of which had a grain of truth. The Greeks saw him as the most terrifying monster ever born, while the Albanians were filled with admiration and pride – there was no other ruler who could compare with him.

He had certainly achieved a great deal. Regions that had previously been terrorised by bandits were swept clean and made accessible. That also benefited merchants, who could now safely travel with their wares, thereby contributing to general prosperity. Like all self-respecting despots, Ali built bridges, laid roads and drained marshes, and built up towns 'without perhaps,' Hobhouse suggests, 'a single other motive than that of his own aggrandisement.' In addition, for the Albanians, he symbolised national unity and the hope of independence from the Turks, to whom he was subordinated in form only. A percentage of the taxes Ali collected were still paid to Constantinople, and he continued to contribute fixed contingents of soldiers to the Sultan's army, but never accepted invitations to visit the Court – he was too fond of his head.

Rumour had it that he was immeasurably rich. He no longer needed to get his hands dirty – the time of plunder was past. Apart from a small war now and again, just to keep his hand in, the majority of his territorial expansion occurred, in Hobhouse's words, 'by the proper disposal of his treasures'. Hobhouse provides a quite detailed summary of Ali's sources of income: 'Of the tenth of all produce collected for the Porte, the Vizier has, at least, a fourth part; he has also near four hundred villages his own property; and, besides, claims from all towns and districts arbitrary sums for protection [how old the mafia is!]. I have seen a computation which sets down his revenues at 6,000,000 of piasters, independent of those casual levies and the presents which are made to him by his Christian subjects. Add to this, that all his work is done gratis, and his kitchens and stables furnished by the towns where he has any establishment.

'He not only gives free quarter to himself and retinue in his numerous expeditions through his dominions, but his soldiers, who only receive about twelve piasters a month from him, are found in bread and meat wherever they go by the inhabitants of the towns and villages ; so that he is able to reserve much of his money for emergencies, for bribing the ministers of the Porte, and buying his neighbours' territories. He is not at much expense in purchasing the male or female slaves of his household; for with these he furnishes himself from the families of the robbers whom he executes or compels to fly. We overtook a man carrying to Tepellenè a boy and girl, who had been just found in the cottage of a robber.'

I have never seen such a minutely detailed description of how the feudal system worked, how its tentacles reached out in all directions into even the smallest country hamlet. Ali did not invent the system; in a wide variety of variants, it was the dominant form of social organisation for many centuries – from Nebuchadnezzar, via the Pharaohs, to Charlemagne and the Russian Tsars. Under the latter it perhaps reached its highest – or lowest – point as serfs remained the property of the landowners even after their deaths, at least if we are to believe Gogol in *Dead Souls*.

Hobhouse does his utmost not to pass moral judgment on Ali Pasha. He believes it would be unfair and unrealistic to judge him by English ethical standards. The methods Ali employed to tame this race of robbers were, he assumed, necessary to force them to respect him and accept his authority, and to guarantee peace and security in his territories.

'What do the Albanians think of Ali Pasha now?' I asked Karagjozi, expecting that the Pasha would be ranked along with Enver Hoxha and other despots.

'We have three great heroes in Albania,' the Professor replied, raising his voice as he always did when his chest swelled with pride. 'Skanderberg, the medieval freedom fighter, Ali Pasha, and Mother Teresa. Ali Pasha Tepelene was a real Albanian. He did much to make Albania an independent country, and fostered our sense of national identity. His dream was to merge the *pashalik* of Shkodra with that of Ioannina to create one great Albania, uniting the Gegs from the north with the Tosks from the south. He developed his part of Albania, building bridges and forts, establishing schools. He was a great soldier, and a clever politician and diplomat. He was known, with good reason, as the 'Mohammedan Bonaparte' and the 'Lion of Ioannina'. When the Albanians ruled the Greeks in the areas under his control, he supported the Greek rebels and trained their leaders. He reasoned that, if the Greeks succeeded in becoming independent, Albania would automatically be free from Turkish domination.'

'What about his cruelty?' I asked.

'They were different times.'

If feudalism was flourishing under Ali Pasha, in England it was in decline in a manner reminiscent of a Shakespearian tragedy. In an essay on Byron, Shelley and Keats that he wrote to instruct his nephew, the Italian writer Giuseppe Tomasi di Lampedusa describes the crisis affecting the country when Byron departed in a packet boat in 1809, watching with increasing joy as the coast disappeared into the distance. Good Old England was in the grip of an economic, political and religious crisis that would change it for good.

At the beginning of the 18th century, a large landowner was absolute lord and master of his estate, the revenue from which flowed not only into his purse but also into the state coffers. By the end of the century, however, it was by far more lucrative to own shares in a factory or in the British East India Company. Being a landowner had become a burden rather than a source of income. That applied too to the estates Lord Byron inherited. Rochdale was bankrupt, and Newstead Abbey was in an advanced state of disrepair. Byron put them in the hands of an agent and left the country. That relieved him of the worry – once he lived in Italy, all he was concerned about was selling the properties.

The nobility, who had always been in control in Parliament, now had to share power more and more with the new industrialist and working classes. On top of this King George III had gone insane and his eight sons had bad reputations. The King, who ate grass and herbs and played Handel on his piano, was interned in Windsor

Castle and his eldest son, the Prince of Wales, took over the government as Regent. But the status of the Royal Family had deteriorated drastically. The princes were all as bad as each other, and the most horrific rumours surrounded them. They were all bigamists and had enormous debts. One of them was reputed to have killed his servant, another was so sadistic towards his soldiers that he could no longer function as a military leader, a third had devoted himself to sexual assault, a fourth had an incestuous relationship with his sister. And, to cap it all, they all quarrelled with each other.

As the people turned their backs on the degenerate Royals, a power struggle was underway in Parliament. The Liberals demanded a new electoral system, equal political rights for Catholics and abolition of the tax on corn, which was detrimental to landowners.

On returning to England after his Grand Tour, Byron chose the moderate, aristocratic Whigs, whose company he preferred. Yet, in his opinions, he was actually more at home with the Radicals – though, according to Leslie Marchand, aristocratic pride prevented him from openly allying himself with their leaders. During his youth in Scotland, when he and his mother lived in poor circumstances and he played with children from simple backgrounds, he had developed a lifelong sympathy with the 'people'.

He took his seat in Parliament, with the possibility of a political career in the back of his mind, and prepared a speech. He intended to make a plea in support of the stocking weavers of Nottingham, who had rebelled in protest against their working conditions. The Tory government had ordered signs to be hung up warning that anyone who broke a weaving frame would be risking the death penalty. Although Byron had confidence in his powers of oratory and persuasion, when it came to it he was very apprehensive. Perhaps he was unconsciously aware that, by calling for an improvement in the lot of the stocking weavers, he was undermining his own chances of a political career, before it had even got off the ground. Marchand calls it a 'fatalistic anticipation of the failure of his Parliamentary career, arising partly from self-distrust and partly from a realistic conception of the inexorable degradation of political life.'

His speech left no room for interpretation. His direct attack on the unjust measures of the Tories convinced only the Radicals, who enthusiastically spoke of the best speech by a lord since 'the Lord knows when'.

Yet, sometimes, his curiosity and vanity got the better of his

Jacobin sympathies. These were his main reasons for wishing to visit Ali Pasha, and when back in England he had the opportunity to be introduced to the Prince Regent – an invitation to meet a prince! – he did not refuse, despite being an opponent of the Prince. The Prince, for his part, found it interesting to meet the author of *Childe Harold*. They had a pleasant conversation about literature and discovered a shared admiration for Sir Walter Scott.

Byron also felt that it was necessary to reform Parliament. An outspoken Radical, Major John Cartwright, had collected petitions in favour of reform, until the army made it impossible for him to continue. This was the topic of Byron's second and last speech in which he defended Cartwright's 'petition for the right to petition'. His only supporter was Earl Stanhope, an out-and-out Jacobin. Byron knew that he had signed his own death sentence as far as a political career was concerned.

Yet he remained fascinated by politics throughout his life, especially Rousseau's concept of freedom. An oppressed people fighting for independence could always count on his help. He did not hesitate for a moment when the Italian Carbonari called on him to help them in their resistance to the Austrian regime – and some years later, he fought for the Greek cause.

At the same time, he was fascinated by heroism. He had great admiration for Napoleon and he was not averse to the idea of returning to politics to do something worthwhile and effective. In 1822, he wrote to his friend Thomas Moore: 'The truth is, my dear Moore, you live near the *stove* of society, where you are unavoidably influenced by its heat and its vapours. [...] One thing *only* might lead me back to it, and that is, to try once more if I could do any good in politics; but *not* in the petty *politics* I see now preying upon our miserable country.'

There was also a religious crisis in that 'miserable country'. More and more priests left the official Anglican church in protest against degeneracy and corruption. The best jobs were divided among the members of the elite without any regard for their spiritual qualities; many of these pseudo-clerics paid someone to fulfil their religious duties while they went off hunting. The rebel priests called for reform of the church and a revival of pure faith. Their protests and proposals found widespread support among the people, and the movement led to the founding of the Methodist church, which was particularly popular among the workers in the new industrial regions of the country. The more developed critics called for a radical break with religion. Long before Nietzsche, they wrote anti-religious pamphlets and united in the 'Atheists' Club'.

Shelley, as an anarchist and an atheist, was in many ways a child of his age. Byron's attitude to religion was more ambiguous. Although he criticised and mocked Christianity on countless occasions, there are also clear suggestions of doubt. He was more an agnostic than an atheist. And he had a weakness for the outward display of pomp and circumstance, and for the mysticism, of the Catholic church – it better fitted his temperament than the no-nonsense approach of atheism.

In another letter to Moore, written four days later, his attitude to Christendom – a curious mixture of scepticism, longing and humour – is clear: 'As I said before, I am really a great admirer of tangible religion; and am breeding one of my daughters a Catholic, that she may have her hands full. It is by far the most elegant worship, hardly excepting the Greek mythology. What with incense, pictures, statues, altars, shrines, relics and the real presence, confession, absolution, – there is something sensible to grasp at. Besides, it leaves no possibility of doubt; for those who swallow their Deity, really and truly, in transubstantiation, can hardly find anything else otherwise than easy of digestion.

'I am afraid that this sounds flippant, but don't mean it to be so; only my turn of mind is so given to taking things in the absurd point of view, that it breaks out in spite of me every now and then. Still, I do assure you that I am a very good Christian. Whether you will believe me in this, I do not know; [...]'

Where mockery dominates in this letter, in Byron's journal from the same period – two years before his death – he records serious reflections on the nature of faith. He is convinced that the sprit is eternal, but does not believe in reincarnation or a place of eternal torment like hell: 'I cannot help thinking that the *menace* of Hell makes as many devils, as the severe penal codes of inhuman humanity make villains [...]'.

Now and again, Rousseau's influence can be detected: 'Man is born *passionate* of body, with an innate though secret tendency to the love of Good in his Mainspring of Mind.' But then his sense of reality takes over: 'But God help us all! It is at present a sad jar of atoms.'

Looking back at Byron's way of thinking from our time, you could say that, balancing between Plato and quantum physics, he ultimately comes out somewhere near Einstein's 'God does not play dice'. 'Things must have had a beginning: and what matters it *when* and *how?* I sometimes think that man may be the relic of some higher material being wrecked in a former world, and degenerated in the hardship and struggle through chaos into conformity [...]. But even then, this higher pre-Adamite suppositious creation must have had an origin and a Creator; for a creator is a more natural imagination than a fortuitous concourse of atoms: all things remount to a fountain, though they may flow to an ocean.'

But perhaps Byron's most preposterous, funniest and perhaps most profound statement about religion was: 'I am always most religious upon a sun-shiny day[...].'


THE COUNTRY THAT BYRON FLED in 1809 was in a state of great confusion. Although a new age was dawning with the rapid rise of industry, the fall of the aristocracy and the beginnings of secularisation, in moral terms England remained for a long time in the grip of Puritanism and hypocrisy – the Victorian age was yet to come. Homosexuality had been punishable by death since 1533, though it was rare for anyone to end up on the gallows.

All this had an impact on Byron. Although he was attached to and proud of his aristocratic descent, he was also strongly attracted to 'the common man' – not to mention 'the common woman' – and sympathised with the working classes. A free-thinker when it came to religion he had, as we have seen, vague convictions with a preference for Catholicism. Although, in terms of sexual morals, he was ahead of his time and in practice surrendered to what we would now call free love – in both its homosexual and heterosexual variants – he had to combat the persistent remnants of the prevailing morals within himself. He was exceptionally shocked when his marriage to Annabella Millbanke foundered after only a year, and his love for other boys during his schooldays filled him with a sense of having done things 'about which he was unable to speak', things that were part of the reason he wished to leave the country.

His attitude to women lagged far behind his progressive tendencies. He had an aversion to intellectual women, unless they were famous and elevated above all doubt, like Madame de Staël. He accused Annabella Millbanke, who was mathematically gifted and analysed her husband thoroughly during the single year of their marriage, of being cool and rational. He preferred lovers who remained close to their 'feminine nature', capricious and emotional, women who he could call 'wild animals' and from whom, for the same reasons, he could easily disentangle himself after the enchantment was broken. In fact, despite the fact that he was capable of spontaneous adoration, his attitude to women could be summed up as: '*Soit belle en tais toi*'.

This young, self-willed lord, who bore the seeds of a new age within him, travelled light-heartedly and somewhat naively through a thoroughly feudal country with morals that dated back to the Stone Age, and allowed himself to be enthralled by the splendour of stolen riches, which were more reminiscent of the Middle Ages than the budding industrial era. The attraction of such areas is poignantly expressed by Evelyn Waugh in his travelogue *Ninety-Two Days*: 'One does not travel, any more than one falls in love, to collect material. It is simply part of one's life. For myself and many better than me, there is a fascination in distant and barbarous places, and particularly in the borderlands of conflicting cultures and states of development, where ideas, uprooted from their traditions, become oddly changed in transplantation. It is there that I find the experiences vivid enough to demand translation into literary form.'

Few foreign travellers preceded Lord Byron into Ali Pasha's land. One of them was François de Pouqueville, a doctor in Napoleon's expedition to Egypt. In 1798, bad health forced him to return home prematurely, but his ship was attacked by pirates from Tripoli. As the prisoner of the Bey of Navarino, however, he was free to travel at will. The shock had clearly cured him, and he certainly took advantage of the opportunity to take a good look around. He later described the customs and traditions of the Greeks and Turks in a series of books. From 1805 he spent ten years as general consul at Ali Pasha's court in Ioannina. The fact that neither Hobhouse nor Byron mention him suggests that they never met him. But Hobhouse was familiar with de Pouqueville's work, referring to him frequently in his journal as an authority whose opinions he examined critically.

In Ioannina Byron did meet William Leake, who was then English resident at Ali Pasha's court. Leake had been sent to Constantinople as a military aide, but had enough free time to travel through the Peloponnesus, northern Greece and Asia Minor. After returning to England, he wrote a series of topographic books on these regions, which are now interesting only for their historical value, offering exact descriptions of the original landscape not yet despoiled by a modern road network, urbanisation, industrialisation or tourism. If

Byron found Hobhouse a stickler for detail in his descriptions, Leake was a complete monomaniac who was continually making measurements with a sextant and theodolite, and noted the exact time of everything he did. In *Travellers to an Antique Land* Robert Eisner notes that Leake, sitting on a horse, viewed the land 'from eight or nine feet', as opposed to the 'five to six feet of a walker's eye level or the four-and-a-half-feet of a motorist's'.

I myself had discovered, to my surprise, that eight to nine feet was indeed a very pleasant, perhaps even ideal, height to view the landscape.

# Chapter 16

M Y DEAR GEORGE, it was raining in Tepelene. The city looked even more gloomy and shabby than it had the previous day. Rainwater streaked down the faded plaster of the high-rise flats.

We left the hotel, umbrellas open, and walked down muddy streets to the city centre. I was getting closer to the place that had been fixed in my mind since the day I read your letter to your mother and this whole adventure started. A sentence from the letter kept running through my head: 'I shall never forget the singular scene on entering Tepaleen at five in the afternoon as the Sun was going down, it brought to my recollection (with some change of *dress* however) Scott's description of Branksome Castle [...].'

But it was morning and Tepelene, under a veil of rain, looked as though the sun would never shine there again. Every step brought me closer to the palace of Ali Pasha, the image of your arrival in my mind's eye. Away, 20th century, I muttered as though it were a prayer. Away, nine decades of the 19th century. Please take me back to the autumn of 1809.

We found one of the old entrance gateways, which was high and arched, and through which three horsemen could easily have ridden side-by-side. It was not right that we passed through on foot, with something as banal as an umbrella in our hands. Our entrance lacked all grandeur.

Hobhouse described your arrival as follows: 'The court at Tepel-lenè, which was enclosed on two sides by the palace, and on the other two sides by a high wall, presented us at our first entrance with a sight something like what we might have, perhaps, beheld some hundred years ago in the castle-yard of a great Feudal Lord. Soldiers, with their arms piled against the wall near them, were assembled in different parts of the square: some of them pacing slowly backwards and forwards, and others sitting on the ground in groups. Several horses, completely caparisoned, were being led about, whilst others were neighing under the hands of the grooms. In the part farthest from the dwelling, preparations were made for the feast of the night; and several kids and sheep were being dressed by cooks who were themselves half-armed. Everything wore a most martial look, though not exactly in the style of the head-quarters of a Christian general; for many of the soldiers were in the most common dress, without shoes, and having more wildness in their air and manner than the Albanians we had before seen.'

'For dust thou art, and unto dust shalt thou return.' I know it is true, but it is a great injustice. Although the high battlements surrounding Ali Pasha's citadel were still there, where the palace had once stood with a gallery in front of it, a brown and grey speckled pig was rolling around in the mud. Between clumps of weeds, heaps of rubbish and crude attempts at vegetable gardens, there were a few simple cottages, themselves ancient and ready to return to dust. No delicious aromas betraying preparations for the feast of the night, no babbling fountain. We wandered along bumpy paths with loose stones, through puddles of water, each of us sunk in our disconsolate thoughts about the violence of history and the finitude of everything.

We were now walking along the inside of the battlements, in the hope of finding the gateway on the river side of the citadel where you had entered and where, according to Karagjozi, Ali Pasha's name was carved in the stone. In the walls were remnants of stables, barracks and store-rooms. The remains of Byzantine walls also showed that Ali had built his palace on the site of a much older fort.

With the exception of the pig and a few undernourished dogs, we saw no signs of life at all. The Blue Guide reports that, in 1991, a German couple had almost been murdered within these walls. I knew nothing more about the incident – someone had told me about it, with the best of intentions, just before I left for Albania. Now, as I walked around, I wondered why the attempt had failed. It was the ideal place to rob and kill someone, with only the odd animal as a witness. And it fitted in perfectly with the tradition of bloodshed associated with this place.

Where were they, the Albanians in their '*white kilt*, gold worked cloak, crimson velvet gold laved jacket & waistcoat, silver mounted pistols & daggers [..]'? Where were the 'Tartars with their high caps', the Turks in their 'pelises & turbans', the 'soldiers & black slaves', the 'couriers entering or passing out with the dispatches', the 'boys calling the hour from the minaret of the mosque [...]'?

The rough, yet refined life of Oriental splendour had evaporated, gone up in smoke, erased from the face of the earth as though it had never existed. And you had never been so close, and yet so far away.

A young man emerged from one of the hovels. What is it like living in place where...? The question was on the tip of my tongue. But he came towards us with the same indestructibly cheerful expression on his face as the Canadian we had met the day before. And indeed, he proved to be an Englishman from the same indeterminate church. He was surprised to see us stumbling through the rain in the slum where he was doing social work. We explained that what had brought us there was the quest for a compatriot of his, who had visited Ali Pasha two centuries earlier.

'Ah yes,' he exclaimed, his eyes lighting up. 'He was quite a character....!' At first I thought he meant you, but he was talking about Ali Pasha, who he called 'a real pornographer'.

A pornographer? That was new to us. A man without mercy, yes. A sadist, perhaps. But a pornographer?

Chortling, the missionary told us that Ali Pasha had collected all the pornographic stories of his time, and hired people to write new ones for him. He also took all the most beautiful local girls for himself.

I was not impressed. Compared to roasting opponents alive, an interest in pornographic stories seemed quite an innocent tendency. The fact that we were given this information unsolicited, while we as it were stood on holy ground, said more about the missionary and the church he represented than Ali Pasha. The sermons in their improvised temple were probably peppered with tales of Sodom and Gomorrah – I sympathised with the unsuspecting Albanians who dared to enter and found themselves subjected to that onslaught.

Instead of responding to his accusations we asked him if he knew where the gateway was on the river-side of the citadel. Of course, he knew the place like the back of his hand. He led the way with a spring in his step. How did these young men manage to stay so light-hearted? It was very ironic that a compatriot of yours had to show us the gate through which you had passed. When we found it, this gateway, too, proved to be a tunnel through the thick battlement walls, which – when it came to it – were of no use at all.

Outside the gateway, a wide panoramic view across the Drino

suddenly revealed itself. The river was indeed as wide as the Thames, counting the sandbanks – Hobhouse had not exaggerated. A long wooden suspension bridge resting on stone pillars and accessible only to pedestrians linked the two banks of the river. Karagjozi told us about Ali Pasha's fruitless attempts to preserve the stone arched bridge that had once stood here. But the stone pillars were built on quicksand and could not withstand the combination of high water and storms that turned the river into a roaring torrent. The Pasha may have succeeded in engaging talented writers of pornographic stories, but he never did find an engineer who was able to solve this problem for him.

'Look!' The Englishman pointed to a hamlet on a mountainside on the other side of the river. 'That is where Ali Pasha was born.' We all stared at the same, hardly visible point without becoming any the wiser. The wind was strong and cold. The panorama across the river was beautiful and yet depressing – it was raining and we knew too much about the past.

The missionary cheerfully took his leave and went back into the citadel. He had hardly disappeared when the Professor erupted with anger at his accusations about Ali Pasha. 'None of it is true,' he said, indignantly. 'I have read everything that has ever been written about Ali Pasha, including the many rumours and myths that are in circulation – after all, he was a man who appealed to the imagination – but what that half-wit Englishman said I have never heard before and I refuse to believe it.'

Daniël and I looked at each other and grinned. It was of no interest to us if Ali Pasha had a preference for pornography or not, but it seemed as though, for the Professor, the virginity of Albania was at stake. Daniël turned and looked at the archway above the gateway. The stone with Ali's name had disappeared – it seemed to have been chiselled out quite neatly. Everything that referred to Ali Pasha in any way had been thoroughly erased. Yet no one had been able to prevent the lively memories of the three evenings that he had entertained himself in the company of a pair of young English travellers from being recorded for posterity in the letters and journals they had left behind. They preserved for us a glimpse of Ali Pasha as he had been and preserved fragments of conversations that took place here, where a pig now lived.

You needed only to open Hobhouse's account to see Ali's pleasing, round face with the 'blue quick eyes' and his long white beard which, unlike the majority of his countrymen, he did not continually stroke or sniff at. He was dressed soberly, with the exception of his turban, which was composed of many small rolls of fine gold muslin, and his long dagger, which was studded with brilliants. He was actually quite childish in his boasting, we would think now. Otherwise, why would he be so proud of showing off his weapons? He showed you his pistols, a sabre and a mountain howitzer, and told you that he had several large cannons. A gift from Napoleon was not showy enough, so he had it ornamented himself. During the first evening of your audience, he kept looking through his telescope and eventually asked you to take a look, at a well-chosen moment when a party of Turks on horseback were approaching the city, saying: 'That man whom you see on the road is the chief minister of my enemy Ibrahim Pasha, and he is now coming over to me, having deserted his master to take the stronger side.'

You could almost smell the aroma of the pipes and the coffee, and feel a little sick at the abundance of sweetmeats you were offered. You could hear Ali laughing heartily through the splashing of the fountain – and see Hobhouse's surprise, as such behaviour was 'very uncommon in a man of consequence; I never saw another instance of it in Turkey.' How you must have enjoyed being surrounded by young men in Albanian costumes with hair flowing halfway down their backs and who refilled your pipes three times.

What did you talk about? 'There are no common topics of discourse between a Turkish Vizier and a traveller which can discover the abilities of either party, especially as these conversations are always in the form of question and answer,' says Hobhouse. That is why you did not respond so much to Ali's words as to his manner, which was lively and relaxed. And yet you did manage to exchange worthwhile information, and the Secretary was kept busy translating everything. War was of course, a favoured topic of conversation between men. Fourteen days earlier, the English had taken Zante, Cephalonia, Ithaca and Cerigo, and Ali congratulated his guests on these victories: 'He said he was happy to have the English for his neighbours; that he was sure they would not serve him as the Russians and French had done, in protecting his runaway robbers; that he had always been a friend to our nation, even during our war with Turkey, and had been instrumental in bringing about the peace.'

You and Hobhouse played along, returning courteous compliments. When Ali asked you why you were travelling through

Albania, you buttered him up by replying: '[...] the desire of seeing such a great man as himself.' Hobhouse continues: '"Ay," returned he. "Did you ever hear of me in England?" We, of course, assured him that he was a very common subject of conversation in our country; and he seemed by no means inaccessible to the flattery.'

In passing, you also discussed the siege of Berat. A messenger came rushing in with a letter and a little later, someone came in with a hunting rifle. When you asked if there were many wild fowl in the neighbourhood, Ali told you that the gun was to be sent to Berat to strengthen the firepower of the Vizier's army. You found it impossible not to smile at this 'war in miniature'.

On the last evening, Ali showed an interest in your return journey. He told you in detail which routes were safe and which not, and promised to issue orders to his military posts to provide you with guards if you had to pass through any dangerous areas. He would also order his Governor in Prevesa to send you to Patras in an armed galleon. In that ship, you were to find yourselves in a terrible storm, but you had no inkling of that as you sat quietly by the fountain: 'Fletcher yelled after his wife, the Greeks called on all the saints, the Musselmans on Alla, the captain burst into tears [...].'

Ali also gave you a letter of recommendation to his son Veli Pasha, and then asked if there were anything else you wished: 'We only asked permission to take our Albanian Vasilly to attend us whilst in Turkey, which he readily granted, and asked where the man was. On being informed that he was at the chamber door, he sent for him, and accordingly Vasilly entered; and, though with every proper respect, still was not embarrassed, but, with his hand on his left breast, answered the Vizier's questions in a firm and fluent manner. Ali called him by his name, and asked him why, being at the door, he had not come in to see him ? "For you know, Vasilly," added he, "I should have been glad to have seen you!" He then told him that he was to attend us, and see that we wanted nothing, and talked a good deal to him about the different stages of our route, summing all up by telling him, in a jocose way, that, if any accident happened to us, he would cut off his head; and that we were to write, mentioning how he had behaved. Shortly after this, and having agreed to give his Highness some relation of our travels by letter, we withdrew, and took our last leave of this singular man.'

'AND WHO ARE YOU, might I ask?' said Ali Pasha. I had disguised myself as a man because otherwise I would never have been able to attend your audience.

'I am an emissary from the kingdom of Holland,' I replied, making a deep bow. 'And I have come here from the end of the 20th century to, by your leave, see your honoured guest Lord Byron from close by, and to hear his voice. I have followed him through Epirus and the Lunxheris mountains, but he was always a day ahead of me. Now I have finally caught up with him and I ask nothing more than to observe him from the corner of the room. My second objective was to see you. I am fascinated by lovable but cruel rulers – perhaps I am suffering from Bluebeard syndrome. Since your time, the world has seen many of them come and go, you could fill a chamber of horrors with them, a long wailing wall full of Niches of Shame. To name but a few: Uncle Joe Stalin who looks so trustworthy in his photographs, smiling under his moustache; Adolf Hitler, who was so kind to children and dogs; Idi Amin, the continual joker; the deeply religious Ayatollah Khomeini, who sent children into the minefields... And not to forget your successor, more than a century later, Enver Hoxha, about whom a Dutch newspaper wrote: "On the one hand, a dyed-in-the-wool Stalinist who rigorously cut off his country from the outside world, on the other hand, cultivated, charming in his dealings with people, intelligent, an intellectual, a lover of theatre, philosophy and literature".'

It fell uncomfortably silent when I finished talking. You could hear the water from the fountain falling back into the basin. You raised your eyebrows, surprised, indifferent – I was just another of the curiosities here at the court.

'I do not remember inviting you,' said the Vizier coolly. 'There is something strange about this. Do you know what we do with uninvited guests?' He drew contentedly on his pipe. I shook my head. 'We skin them using the sharpest shells we can find on the seashore.'

'Please don't go to any trouble,' I said hastily. 'I will dissolve into thin air before you can even notice it, and it will be as though I were never here.'

No sooner said than done. You may all have looked in astonishment at the place where, only a moment before, I had stood talking; but then you would have continued your conversation, forgetting my appearance immediately.

WE STARTED TO GO DOWNHILL towards the river, leaving you behind with Ali Pasha. I walked away, out of your letter, and out of Hobhouse's journal. Everything that could have been a reminder of Ali Pasha within the citadel had been destroyed; there was nothing to connect me to 1809.

All that remained was what had been written about you. You died from a cataclysmic combination of marsh fever, bloodletting and goodwill; your body was buried in Newstead Abbey and your heart in Missolonghi. Ali Pasha was felled by a bullet that passed through the floor and penetrated his back. His body was buried in the citadel in Ioannina, from where, long ago, it was stolen – an appropriate fate for a dead robber, in my opinion. His head was displayed for some time in Constantinople (in those days, they used to drag body parts all over the place): 'For two hours, Ali Pasha's head had been on display in the Niche of Shame. Paler than usual in the new dark suit he had had fitted for his wedding, Abdullah stood in his usual place, hands behind his back, staring at the crowds of people flooding the square. After the niche had been empty for several days (the head of Bugrhan Pasha had been removed five days previously), it was once again as busy as always on the square. On headless days, the square created a bemused, unnatural, unsettled impression. The crowd shuffled blind and aimlessly across the pavement. The square had lost its equilibrium. But now that it had a new head, it had returned to normal. The flow of people seemed ordered by a certain regularity, that made Abdullah think of the tides of the sea under the influence of the moon. The head on the edge of the square fulfilled the same role as a guardian angel.'

This is how Ismail Kadare described the history of Ali Pasha's head in *The Niche of Shame*. The Sultan had made many fruitless attempts to call Ali to order: 'A few months ago, on the eve of his departure (the wind was howling exactly as it is today), he had gone to the high, cold halls of the National Archives to study the documents on Ali Pasha. He had spent hours bent over the letters exchanged between the Sultan and the Vizier of Albania. The intervals between the letters became longer and longer. The last of them, it seemed to him, could only be read to the accompaniment of the disconsolate howling wind that made the high windows of the Archives rattle. "I appeal to you one last time," wrote the Sultan. "If you do not obey me this time, know that I will destroy you with fire and sword. To ash, I will reduce you to ash." That was indeed the final letter. There was no reply from Ali. At incredible speeds, the couriers had covered the distance between the two continents with nothing but emptiness in their bags. Winter approached. The exchange of letters came to a stop. After the letters, it was a matter of waiting for the ravens, for the gunpowder.'

Before they destroyed Ali's palaces, the Sultan's soldiers had sought in vain for the Pasha's legendary treasure, that was reputed to have been stored in the palace in Tepelene. Hobhouse also mentioned it: 'In this palace it is reported that Ali preserves the greatest part of his treasure, and, if you believe the Albanians, some of the inner rooms are piled up to the top with jewels and coin.'

I felt expelled from history. Suddenly the past had receded, and I was sent back to the end of the second millennium – which, too, would soon be over. Everything passed. Even the moment at which we wandered around the citadel searching in vain for the remains of the palace was already in the past. That the present is, only a second later, part of the past gave me a sense of haste – you had to grasp as much as possible, everything blew away in your hands in the whirling tornado of time. Committing events to paper was a desperate attempt to force time to stand still for a moment, but it was to no avail. The story of our journey would never be the same as the journey itself.

The others stood halfway down the path, bending over three newborn puppies that had been tossed alive from the battlements – the way to dispose of all rubbish in Albania. They squeaked and wriggled. Daniël used a rock to put them out of their misery. We stepped over the little bodies and walked further downhill. A cruel wind blew into our faces from the direction of the river.

Now I no longer had you both to put everything into a favourable perspective, I was no longer protected from the desolation of Tepelene. There was a sense of dread that I could not explain and which gave me an oppressive feeling that all the ordeals that the Albanians had been subjected to over the centuries were not yet over. I could hear a low growling – it seem to come from deep in the throats of the inhabitants. I was privileged, I could leave again. Like a migratory bird, I had passed over one corner of the country, had inhaled the air and could now, wings flapping, return to my breeding ground.

We walked past a field where a sheep had just been slaughtered. The animal hung upside down on a pole while two men removed its skin. Underfed dogs lurked, ready to pounce. All around, the grass was strewn with the bones of sheep – a valley of bones at the foot of Ali's citadel.

Without you the enchantment was broken, the magic was gone. I could only follow my own trail – back to where I came from. If I stayed here, I would end up like Ali Pasha's donkey, about which the following story was told: it was the donkey's job to fetch water for Ali, together with a donkey-man, from the village of Valare. It did this for years and became so accustomed to it that, when Ali died, it carried on, alone. People would say to the donkey: 'Stupid ass, you should forget about Valare, Ali Pasha is dead.' This became a widely used expression for someone who indulged too much in nostalgia and, against their own better judgment, continued to long for a time when they were happy or for something wonderful that they could not forget.

While I was writing the story of my journey, I too became very much like Ali's donkey. I kept on fetching water, deaf to what people said to me, to questions like: Who in God's name is interested in Lord Byron? Why Albania, of all places? Gradually I realised that the purpose of the journey was not you, or Ali Pasha's palace, but the actual process of travelling to Tepelene, with you as a shadow, always at a suitable distance ahead of me. To place myself with you (such vanity) in a single past, even though it was a past that lasted only eight days – a stolen, voyeuristic and one-sided intimacy of which you would have remained unaware if I had not addressed myself directly to you in these letters.

# Epilogue

Yet oft-times in his maddest mirthful mood
Strange pangs would flash along Childe Harold's brow,
As if the memory of some deadly feud
Or disappointed passion lurk'd below:
But this none knew, nor haply cared to know;
For his was not that open, artless soul
That feels relief by bidding sorrow flow,
Nor sought he friend to counsel or condole,
Whate'er this grief mote be, which he could not control.

Back in ioannina, a week after his visit to Ali Pasha, Byron started to write the great epic poem *Childe Harold's Pilgrimage*. Two years later, when he returned to London, the first two cantos were finished. He gave them, together with other manuscripts for which he had much higher expectations, to a friend for possible publication. Of the two cantos he said: 'They are not worth troubling you with, but you shall have them all with you, if you like.' His friend read the manuscript and was baffled. He wrote to Byron immediately, saying: 'You have written one of the most delightful poems I ever read.' He implored Byron to publish it, and the latter eventually agreed, but only after he had made a few changes.

Where Hobhouse had recorded their shared adventures during the Grand Tour in his journal with more scientific than literary ambitions, Byron – who until then had written no poetry of note – spontaneously created his own new form for a long, autobiographical poem in Spenserian stanzas, in which the melancholic hero made an identical journey not only to the traditional centres of classical cultures, but also to as yet unknown, but no less fascinating, countries like Portugal, Spain, Epirus and Albania.

The poem was an immediate success. English readers were ripe for the poetic tale of a journey through rough, barbaric regions full of bizarre customs and the sensual yet cruel culture of the Orient, the beauty in verse of ruins and palaces, and of Arcadian, spectacular and sinister landscapes. And they were enthralled by the charm of the wandering nobleman, consumed by strange torments, who suffered not only from unrequited love ('He loved only one person but that one could alas never be his!) but also from his own inadequacy and a 'youth squandered on foolish whims'. Historical events, like the Napoleonic wars, play a role in the background, adding to the heroic atmosphere.

And most exhilarating of all: through the whole thing shimmered the persona of the poet himself, who appeared interchangeable with his hero, tormented by introspection and loved by no one. Readers would be hypnotised by the drawn-out regularity of the meter, only to be abruptly aroused by exhortations like 'Lo!' or 'Hark! at the start of a line, hurling them emotionally into the middle of the action. Lampedusa called it 'a malicious music, offering the reader a mixture of irony, tenderness and the experience of life and death'.

The reader happily identifies with the suffering of this English Werther, which is both a poetic pose and a representation of the melancholy that also regularly overtook Byron. Goethe had already noted that the tortures of existence were 'Byron's element; he was always a self-tormentor'. Byron had a Calvinist tendency to feel guilty and to punish himself. He was in the habit of saying 'some curse hangs over me and mine' and he was convinced that he brought bad fortune to anyone who entered into a relationship with him.

That this sense of guilt does not degenerate into self-pity; and pathos in his poetry is due to the fact that, in *Childe Harold*, the melancholy is transferred to the suffering of humanity in general in a world that is far from perfect. The self-pity of Byron's hero acquires a different dimension when it is related to that of other historical and literary figures who have also been the victims of circumstance. His complaints are filled with indirect sympathy. As Francis Berry, in *Byron's Poetry*, says: '...it is this more-than-personal spread of grief or melancholy which makes Byron's lament noble, or, as Francis Jeffrey said in his revision of Canto IV in 1818, "majestic" and "sublime".'

By recounting his journey in literary form in *The Pilgrimage of Childe Harold*, Byron turned his own life into a work of art, and in turn that art influenced his life. Once *Childe Harold* had become such a sensation, England welcomed back its prodigal son with open arms. He was inundated with invitations, prominent women threw themselves into his arms and he drank from the cup until it was dry, until it filled him with disgust. It was in this period that he acquired his reputation as a misanthropist, an *homme fatale*, and a scandalous lover.

Shortly afterwards, translations of *Childe Harold* conquered continental Europe where, partly due to his later works and his death fighting for the Greek cause, his fame endured much longer than in his mother country, where his significance as a poet was soon overshadowed by that of Shelley and Keats.

For a century and a half, he was seen in his own country as a minor poet, whose fame was founded on 'love, orgies and death', in the words of Mario Praz in *The Pact with the Serpent*. Goethe had exclaimed: 'Admirable! Every word is strong, significant, and subservient to the aim; [...] I have hitherto found no weak lines in Byron!' Yet more than a century later, poet and outspoken critic T.S. Eliot said: 'Byron has been admired for what are his most ambitious attempts to sound poetic: and these attempts turn out on closer examination to be fake; nothing but sonorous affirmations of the commonplace.' For Eliot, poetry should be something very concentrated, very distilled – something which, in his opinion, Byron was not capable of. If Byron, he said, had 'distilled his verse, there would have been nothing whatever left.'

And yet there have been many attempts to revalue Byron's work. Francis Berry, educated in the tradition of T.S. Eliot, dilutes the severe opinions of his tutor in his essay 'The Poet of Childe Harold'. He sees Eliot's total rejection of the poet Byron as a necessary standpoint within a process of poetic development that he too underwent, as a result of which his ideal of poetry ended up diametrically opposed to that of Byron. In 1974, Berry dared to cut himself loose from Eliot's domination and re-read Byron without inhibition: 'I have come, and not a moment too soon, to accept Byron's poetry with enormous pleasure and admiration, and to receive, when I read him, an intense kind of driving excitement, vigour and assurance not found elsewhere in nineteenth-century English poetry. And with what consequence? With this: he alone would seem to combine a propulsive revolutionary blaze, an expanding of sympathies, with an equally strong blaze – or passion – for metrical and stanzaic, and a larger constructional order. In the present age of fervour but near anarchy in life and in letters, Byron is the wholesome model for poets writing today, and tomorrow. He admired Dryden; he admired Pope. Yet he was liberal; more than that, a liberator; and he understood himself.'

In his essay, Lampedusa made a selection to separate the corn from the chaff – Byron was, after all, also a playwright, polemist and translator. Lampedusa devoted considerable attention to Byron's final long, epic poem *Don Juan*, which he called 'perfect'. In *Don Juan* Byron finally found his ultimate form, the octave: verses of eight lines, the first six of which lead up to a climax or comment in the last two. As an excellent form for comedy and satire, he finally had an outlet for his humour. In *Don Juan* the plaintive, sometimes almost melodramatic tone of *Childe Harold* makes way for an alternately mocking and melancholic mood, which is light-hearted yet intense. The poet had achieved the distance that permitted him to poke fun at everyone and everything, including himself – as he had always done in his letters and journals. Finally, you could say, he had become himself in his poetry.

READING *CHILDE HAROLD*, it is important to look beyond the archaic language and verse to discover what was then new and exciting. Countries like Spain, Greece and Turkey – which now grace the covers of holiday brochures and are no longer exotic to us – were for those who could not afford a Grand Tour of Arcadian and Oriental fantasy worlds. We see a young nobleman travelling more or less alone through unimaginable, wild regions, which were then still untouched and worth describing. Such a character was very much in fashion – a touch of aristocracy and melancholy, a dash of heroism, a longing for adventure, danger and, if necessary, self-destruction, and then the enchanting doom that hung above his head and seemed to affect everything that his glance happened to fall upon.

Although Childe Harold's state of mind may now seem to us peculiar, there remains the attraction of worlds that are long gone and people who were then still unknown – that have perhaps not changed as much as we might think at first glance. The following stanzas from Canto II of *Childe Harold's Pilgrimage* give an impression of his visit to Ali Pasha:

## Childe Harold Canto II

*LV*

The sun had sunk behind vast Tomerit,
And Laos wide and fierce came roaring by;
The shades of wonted night were gathering yet,
When, down the steep banks winding warily,
Childe Harold saw, like meteors in the sky,
The glittering minarets of Tepalen,
Whose walls o'erlook the stream; and drawing nigh,
He heard the busy hum of warrior-men
Swelling the breeze that sigh'd along the lengthening glen.

*LVI*

He pass'd the sacred Haram's silent tower,
And underneath the wide o'er-arching gate
Survey'd the dwelling of this chief of power,
Where all around proclaim'd his high estate.
Amidst no common pomp the despot sate,
While busy preparation shook the court,
Slaves, eunuchs, soldiers, guests, and santons wait;
Within, a palace, and without, a fort:
Here men of every clime appear to make resort.

*LVII*

Richly caparison'd, a ready row
Of armed horse, and many a warlike store,
Circled the wide extending court below;
Above, strange groups adorn'd the corridore;
And oft-times through the Area's echoing door,
Some high-capp'd Tartar spurr'd his steed away:
The Turk, the Greek, the Albanian, and the Moor,
Here mingled in their many-hued array,
While the deep war-drum's sound announced the close of day.

*LVIII*

The wild Albanian kirtled to his knee,
With shawl-girt head and ornamented gun,
And gold-embroider'd garments, fair to see:
The crimson-scarfed men of Macedon;
The Delhi with his cap of terror on,

And crooked glaive; the lively, supple Greek:
And swarthy Nubia's mutilated son;
The bearded Turk, that rarely deigns to speak,
Master of all around, too potent to be meek,

*LIX*

Are mix'd conspicuous: some recline in groups,
Scanning the motley scene that varies round;
There some grave Moslem to devotion stoops,
And some that smoke, and some that play, are found;
Here the Albanian proudly treads the ground;
Half whispering there the Greek is heard to prate;
Hark! from the mosque the nightly solemn sound,
The Muezzin's call doth shake the minaret,
'There is no god but God! – to prayer – lo! God is great!'

*LX*

Just at this season Ramazani's fast
Through the long day its penance did maintain:
But when the lingering twilight hour was past,
Revel and feast assumed the rule again:
Now all was bustle, and the menial train
Prepared and spread the plenteous board within;
The vacant gallery now seem'd made in vain,
But from the chambers came the mingling din,
As page and slave anon were passing out and in.

*LXI*

Here woman's voice is never heard: apart,
And scarce permitted, guarded, veil'd, to move,
She yields to one her person and her heart,
Tamed to her cage, nor feels a wish to rove:
For, not unhappy in her master's love,
And joyful in a mother's gentlest cares,
Blest cares! all other feelings far above!
Herself more sweetly rears the babe she bears,
Who never quits the breast, no meaner passion shares.

## LXII

In marble-paved pavilion, where a spring
Of living water from the centre rose,
Whose bubbling did a genial freshness fling,
And soft voluptuous couches breathed repose,
ALI reclined, a man of war and woes:
Yet in his lineaments ye cannot trace,
While Gentleness her milder radiance throws
Along that aged venerable face,
The deeds that lurk beneath, and stain him with disgrace.

## LXIII

It is not that yon hoary lengthening beard
Ill suits the passions which belong to youth;
Love conquers age – so Hafiz hath averr'd,
So sings the Teian, and he sings in sooth –
But crimes that scorn the tender voice of ruth,
Beseeming all men ill, but most the man
In years, have mark'd him with a tiger's tooth;
Blood follows blood, and, through their mortal span,
In bloodier acts conclude those who with blood began.

## LXIV

'Mid many things most new to ear and eye
The pilgrim rested here his weary feet,
And gazed around on Moslem luxury,
Till quickly wearied with that spacious seat
Of Wealth and Wantonness, the choice retreat
Of seated Grandeur from the city's noise:
And were it humbler it in sooth were sweet;
But Peace abhorreth artificial joys,
And Pleasure, leagued with Pomp, the zest of both destroys.

## LXV

Fierce are Albania's children, yet they lack
Not virtues, were those virtues more mature.
Where is the foe that ever saw their back?
Who can so well the toil of war endure?
Their native fastnesses not more secure
Than they in doubtful time of troublous need:

Their wrath how deadly! but their friendship sure,
When Gratitude or Valour bids them bleed,
Unshaken rushing on where'er their chief may lead.

Most of all, I like reading Byron's letters and journals. For anyone who might think that the maudlin Childe Harold is identical to Lord Byron, one letter is enough. The writer is a surprisingly down-to-earth and sceptical man. And he possesses a wholesome dose of self-mockery, sometimes to the extreme.

One sentence is enough to determine his tone: 'What have I seen? the same man all over the world, – ay, and woman, too.'

Byron's letters and journal extracts offer a clear image of a vital but restless man who seems to be continually searching for a synthesis between the irreconcilable contrasts in himself and the world around him. 'This journal is a relief. When I am tired ... out comes this, and down goes every thing. But I can't read it over–and God knows what contradictions it may contain. If I am sincere with myself (but I fear one lies more to one's self than to any one else) every page should confute, refute, and utterly abjure its predecessor.'

The desire to be 'sincere' leads to candid revelations in which he spares no one, including himself. He likes to pull out all the stops to give a good tongue-lashing, from foreign parts, to the political and literary establishment in his homeland. He sees himself as an outsider, someone who is neither ready nor willing to take part in what we would now call the rat race: 'I have really no friends in the world; though all my old school companions are gone forth into that world, and walk about there in monstrous disguises, in the garb of guardsmen, lawyers, parsons, fine gentlemen, and such other masquerade dresses.'

Nothing is sacred for Byron. He did not even have a high regard for his own status as a poet and of poetry in general: 'I by no means rank poetry or poets high in the scale of intellect. [...] I prefer the talents of *action* – of war, or the senate, or even of Science [...].'

Although he regularly surrendered himself completely to the 'tumultuous departments of existence', he was at least as frequently overtaken by *taedium vitae*: 'I am *ennuyé* beyond my usual tense of that yawning verb, which I am always conjugating; and I don't find that society much mends the matter. I am too lazy to shoot myself [...].' This death wish has less to do with a then fashionable poetic *Weltschmerz* than with a more contemporary feeling of what Sartre called *La Nausée*. In that sense, Byron is more a 'modern' man than the romantic he is reputed to be.

Some of his letters, devoted to the delights, torments and worries of love, give a clear picture of his ambivalent feelings towards women. If, at the age of 16, I had read these letters rather than an anthology of his most popular poems, the 'Byron myth' in which I so ardently believed would have been viciously shattered.

'There is something to me very softening in the presence of a woman, – some strange influence, even if one is not in love with them – which I cannot at all account for, having no very high opinion of the sex. But yet – I always feel in better humour with myself and every thing else, if there is a woman within ken.'

To Lady Melbourne, an older woman who he held in high esteem and with whom he maintained a Platonic friendship, he wrote: 'I have no very high opinion of your sex, but when I do see a woman superior not only to all her own but to most of ours I worship her in proportion as I despise the rest.'

We would have been able to read his memoires, which he thought were in the safe keeping of his friend Thomas Moore if his widow, Annabella Millbanke, and half-sister Augusta, with whom he had an incestuous relationship, had not thrown them into the fire one rainy evening in July 1824 – ostensibly, with the aim of preserving Byron's reputation after death, but in reality to ensure that they themselves would go down in history with their names unbesmirched.

Byron never devoted himself to writing detailed descriptions of landscapes, architecture or people. His ornate account of his visit to Ali Pasha in the letter to his mother is an exception. He was happy to leave the record of their journey to Hobhouse: 'He [Hobhouse] would potter with map and compass at the foot of Pindus, Parnes, and Parnassus, to ascertain the site of some ancient temple of city. I rode my mule up them. They had haunted my dreams from boyhood; the pines, eagles, vultures, and owls, were descended from those Themistocles and Alexander had seen, and were not degenerated like humans; the rocks and torrents the same. John Cam's dogged perseverance in pursuit of his hobby is to be envied; I have no hobby and perseverance. I gazed at the stars, and ruminated; took no notes, asked no questions.'

After they had completed their journey, Hobhouse returned with full notebooks to England. Byron continued to travel: 'I feel happier, I feel free'. The continual company of Hobhouse, with whom he would remain friends for his entire life, had often caused him great irritation: 'I determined after one years purgatory to part with that amiable soul, for though I like him, and always shall, though I give him almost as much credit for his good qualities as he does himself, there is something in his manner &c. in short he will never be any thing but the "Sow's Ear".'

A year later, Byron completed his Grand Tour. On the way home, he took stock: 'At twenty-three, the best of life is over and its bitters double.' That was a little premature, as life still had much in store for him, but it did testify to a certain foresight. He was to experience much misery: clashes with society, abuse, divorce, and a series of deaths among his family and friends. Immediately after he returned to England, his mother died before he had the opportunity to visit her, and shortly afterwards his dear friend Charles Matthews drowned. Later, he would lose his daughter Allegra, and experience the death of Shelley at close hand.

Yet, at the same time, he used the following words to describe himself: 'I am like the Jolly Miller, caring for nobody, and not cared for.' It was this attitude that made him a survivor. Whatever happened, the next day, he would ride his horse, swim or write a poem. Childe Harold would become Don Juan, that was how it was meant to be.

# Bibliography

Berry, F., 'The Poet of Childe Harold', in: F.D. McConnell (ed.),
   *Byron's Poetry*, New York, Norton 1978

Byron, Lord, *The Complete Poetical*, Oxford, The Clarendon Press
   1980

Eisner, R., *Travelers to an Antique Land: The history and literature
   of travel to Greece*, Ann Arbor, University of Michigan Press 1991

Hobhouse, John Cam, *Journey through Albania and Other Provinces
   of Turkye in Europe and Asia*, London, James Cawthorne 1813

Kadare, Ismail, *De Nis der Schande* (The Niche of Shame),
   Amsterdam, Van Gennep 1990

Kadare, Ismail, *Chronicle in Stone*, New York, New Amsterdam
   Books, 1987

Koster, Daniël, *Griekenland* (Greece), ANWB travel guides, The
   Hague, ANWB 1991

Lampedusa, Giuseppe Tommasi di, *Letteratura inglese* (English
   literature), Milan, Mondadori, 1990

Malamas Lambros, *A Tourist Guide of Epiros*, edited by Mrs. Mary
   French, seventh edition

Marchand, Leslie A. (ed), *Byron's Letters and Journals*, 12 volumes,
   London, John Murray, 1973–1982

Marchand, Leslie A., *Byron: A portrait*, New York, Alfred A. Knopf
   1970

Matzneff, Gabriël, *La diétetique de Lord Byron* (Lord Byron's
   Dietetics), Paris, La Table Ronde 1984

Mulder, Gerda and Piet Ordeman, *Reisgids Albanië* (Albania Travel
   Guide), second edition, Rotterdam, Ordeman 1988

Praz Mario, *Het verdrag met de slang* (The Pact with the Serpent),
   Amsterdam, De Arbeiderspers 1986

**TESSA DE LOO** made her debut in 1983 with *Girls from the Candy Factory* and has appeared in Ellery Queen Mystery Magazine. Her wartime story *The Twins* (1993) was an enormous success in the Netherlands and abroad and has been translated into 22 languages. Haus also published her novel *The Book of Doubt*. Tessa lives in southern Portugal and is one of the most successful writers in the Dutch language.

This edition has been generously supported by the Foundation for the Production and Translation of Dutch Literature

First published in Great Britain in 2010 by
Armchair Traveller at the bookHaus Ltd
70 Cadogan Place
London SW1X 9AH
*www.thearmchairtraveller.com*

A CIP catalogue record for this book is available from the British Library
ISBN 978-1-906598-77-8

Designed and typeset in Garamond by MacGuru Ltd
*info@macguru.org.uk*
Printed and bound in China by 1010 Printing International Ltd